SHARPEN YOUR ACTS!

Christian Life Practice

by Craig Harris

Sharpen Your Acts!
Copyright © 2000, 1998 **Sycamore Tree Publishing Company**
Third Printing
                By Craig Harris

All rights revered. Except for the reproducible student sheets and signs which may be copied for ministry use, no part of this book may be copied without permission from the publisher.

Scripture quotations, unless otherwise indicated, are taken from the *Holy Bible: New International Version.* Copyright © 1973, 1978, 1984 by International Bible Society. Used by permission of Zondervan Publishing House.

Printed in the United States of America ISBN 0-9663783-0-X

The wonderful artwork throughout this book is by Dan Nelson from his book: "Off the Wall - Cartoon Clip Art for Student Ministry"
Copyright © Gene Johnson Productions. All rights reserved. Used by permission

                You Can Order Dan Nelson's
                          book at:
              Gene Johnson Productions, Inc.
                      P.O. Box 1058
                Jonesboro, Georgia, 30237
             1-800-324-4363, 1-770-477-5417
        Fax: 770-477-5427 Email: gjp@inetnow.net

    Special thanks to my wife, Jodi; my children, David and Savannah; my brother, Kevin; my parents, Don and Fran; also, Mike Mynatt, Perry Eaton, Rick Cassells, Danny Dowdy, Robert Rachuig and Walter and Judy Bales.
    This books is dedicated to the students at Westwood Baptist Church in Palestine, Texas, who were the inspiration and guinea pigs in developing this project.   Craig

Cover design and artwork: John Fender © 1998

              Sycamore Tree Publishing Company
     "Climb the Sycamore Tree to see Jesus more clearly"
          www.sycamoretreepublishing.com
            1-888-627-7848 Fax: 1-419-831-9669

SHARPEN YOUR ACTS!
Christian Life Practice

Table of Contents:

Introduction
How to use this Course
Session One: Prayer Practice
Session Two: Testimony Practice
Session Three: Word Study Practice
Session Four: Scripture Memory Practice
Session Five: Worship Practice
Session Six: Bible Study Practice
Session Seven: Self Esteem Practice
Session Eight: Teaching Practice
Session Nine: Obedience Practice
Session Ten: Witnessing Practice

Introduction:

What if a football coach just lectured to his players about how to play the game but never let them get out on the field, knock heads, and practice the plays? The team would lose every game! The Christian walk is much more important than any game. Young people need to practice the tenets of the faith just like they need to practice playing a sport or an instrument.

That's what this book is all about. There *is* an opponent - an enemy - and he wants our young people to lose battles against him every day. Let's equip and prepare them so they can defeat him through God's power.

Sharpen Your Acts! has been tried and proven in hundreds of ministries across the nation - and around the world. You will guide your students as they practice witnessing to each other, sharing their testimonies, praying, worshiping together, teaching, studying chapters, building one another up, and being obedient to God.

Your youth will enjoy being able to participate - instead of just sitting and listening - and you will be amazed at what you see them do. Now, get ready to hear your students pray and see them witness and...

How to use this Course:

The sessions are divided into the following elements:

A Peek at the Practice:
This is an overview of the session.

The Primary Objective Points:
These are the objectives the sessions will cover.

Plan Ahead:
These are simple instructions telling you how to prepare ahead of time for the session. This tells you what materials will be needed and how to set up the room.

Prompt Your Young People:
5 - 10 minutes.
This is how to begin the session. There will be a "prompt question" for the students to answer to begin each session. You will take up the question strips and read them to the students to get them thinking about the topic.

Preface the Practice:
20 - 25 minutes.
This is the introduction to the session's practice topic. Here, you will talk about the topic and prepare your students to practice doing it.

A Promise to Ponder:
A scripture reference pertaining to the session.

Practice Makes Perfect:
25 - 40 minutes.
Here, you will instruct your students on how they will practice this session's topic. The students will then actually practice doing what the session is about. The students will divide into teams in several sessions.

A Post-Practice Postlude:
5 - 10 minutes.
This is the conclusion to the session.

The times are given as a general idea to keep you on track, and will vary from session to session. Each session has more than enough material to last an **hour.** Remember, your students *will* participate if you present the session topics with enthusiasm. You may say, "my students will *never* pray aloud or witness..." Never say "never"! They may just surprise you what they will do if given the chance.

You will need a **copy machine**, pencils and paper for every session. Don't cut pages in this book - make copies of needed pages first, cut along the lines where needed, then make the students' copies.

That way you can use the course over and over again.
Permission is granted to make copies of pages needed for the sessions.

1

Session One: **Prayer Practice**

A Peek at the Practice:

By the end of this session, you will have taught your students the importance of a daily prayer life and will have led them to pray aloud in front of their peers.

The Primary Objective Points:

Students Will:

- Learn the importance of an honest, consistent, daily prayer life.

- Actually practice praying aloud in front of others following the model prayer Jesus gave us.

- Become more comfortable praying both alone and with others.

Plan Ahead:

Read through the lesson plan. Personalize it to fit your group's personality. Make any adjustments you deem necessary to fit the size and makeup of your group.

Make copies of the **prompt** question sheets (Prayer B), then cut them into strips along the dotted lines. Make enough strips for each student. Have pens or pencils ready for each student's use.

Make enough copies of the **Pray with Power** handout sheet (Prayer C) for each student.

Pray for your students and for this session. You must lead your students by example and it would be difficult to teach them to pray if you do not. If you don't pray daily, start now!

Set a chair by the doorway so students will pass by it as they enter. Place the **prompt** questions strips on it. Place the sign "Please take a sheet and answer the question" (Prayer A) on the chair.

Be sure you have room available to send students into separate teams. They will need to be far enough apart from each other so that they will not distract other teams. Use the corners of a larger meeting room, or send individual teams into separate classrooms if they are available.

Make a transparency of **Pray with Power** (Prayer C), or have a dry-erase or chalk board available on which to place its elements.

8

Prompt Your Young People:

As the students enter the room, they will take a strip of paper and answer the question. Take up the strips or have a volunteer do so.

Begin your session time as you are most comfortable: Make needed announcements, sing songs, etc.

Next, take prayer requests. Pray, or call on someone to pray.

Sort through the "question strips" and read a variety of answers to the students. Be careful not to criticize the students' answers: you want them to be honest with you.

Allow for comments on the answers, including letting students comment on their own answers if they so choose.

Make positive comments on prayers that the students say have been answered and explain to them that God does answer prayers and you will be talking about that in this session.

Practice Pointer:
Do students need to sign their names? Not unless they just want to.

Practice Pointer:
Even if they *all* say they have never had a prayer answered, then you know you have some work to do. Don't be discouraged if they just don't realize yet that God does answer prayers.

Practice Pointer:
Consider making a prayer journal for your youth group. Write down prayer requests and be sure to check them off as they are answered.

Preface the Practice:

Ask: "For what purpose did God create us?"

Explain that God created us to *walk* with Him, which means to have fellowship with Him - to talk to Him!
Prayer is what we were created for, so it's the most important thing we can do.
Jesus said, "If you ask *anything* in my name, I will do it." He *wants* us to pray to Him and he *wants* to answer us.

Ask: "So why do we sometimes feel that God doesn't give us exactly what we ask for?"

Explain that praying in His *name* means praying in his *will* and God's *will* is always what's best for us. When we pray for things that will glorify God and help us to be more like Him, *then* we can ask for "mountains to move" and God will move them.

Ask: "What if you asked God, 'in Jesus' name, I want a brand new sports car'. Do you think you would get it?"

Probably not. Again, praying in Jesus' name is not some secret formula for getting anything we want. Praying in Jesus' name means praying for things that *He* wants us to have - because they are good for us - and because they glorify God. Even Paul asked God to remove the "thorn in his side," but God's answer was, "My grace is sufficient for

Practice Pointer:
Some scripture references are:
Genesis 3:8, 5:24, 6:9
Micah 6:8
Revelation 3:20

Practice Pointer:
John 14:14
Also note that James 1:6,7 says we must not *doubt* when we ask or we will not get our prayers answered.

Practice Pointer:
Matthew 17:20

Practice Pointer:
2 Corinthians 12:8,9

you." In other words, God wanted Paul to have that problem, whatever it was.

Why? God said that He, God, would be glorified in Paul's weakness. God wanted Paul to rely on *Him* and not his own strength. We *should* boldly ask God for what we *want*, and as we get closer and closer to Him, we will find more and more of our prayers answered.

Jesus also taught that we should not give up, but keep on praying for what we want or need.

Practice Pointer:
Luke 18: 1 - 8 is the story of the persistent widow who got what she wanted because she kept asking the judge.

Ask: "What kind of relationship would a guy and girl have if they never spoke to each other? Would that be a good or bad relationship?"

Explain that it is impossible to have a good relationship with God if we never talk with Him. Again, He wants us to *walk* with Him, and that means to communicate with Him, to fellowship with Him. To pray.

Practice Pointer:
How does God speak to us? Primarily through His spirit as we pray, through the Bible and through preaching and teaching.

Ask: "Paul said we should 'pray all the time', so does that mean we should walk around school or the mall with our eyes closed, praying to God?"

Practice Pointer:
1 Thessalonians 5:17

Explain that we should be in an *attitude* of prayer - where we feel God's presence all the time and realize that He is there. We should access His power and grace in all situations and we should pray about everything: every decision, every problem, even every good thing. And, no, we don't need to always close our eyes to pray. We do that so we can shut out distractions when we are able - like at church or before a meal. God can read our minds, so we don't have to pray aloud all the time either - that would be quite a sight!

Practice Pointer:
Jesus said in **Matthew 6:6** to go to a quiet place to pray, alone with the Father. We can't stay *all* the time in a "prayer closet", but we should spend *some* time there.

Ask: "Have you ever been mad at God? If so, do you think you should tell Him - or keep it to yourself out of respect for Him?"

Explain that we *can't* keep things to ourselves when it comes to God. He already knows when we are mad at Him. So be honest with Him, He is big enough to handle it. Sure, sometimes we get mad at Him, but He wants us to approach Him like a child would a loving father - to crawl up in His lap and call him "daddy". God already knows what you are thinking, so be honest with Him - but always with proper respect; after all, He *is* God!

Practice Pointer:
Romans 8:15. *Abba* is equivalent to *daddy*.

So how do we pray? Jesus gave us a model prayer in Matthew 6:9-13. **Read this passage with your students - or have them quote this "Lord's prayer" together. Take time to have your students memorize the prayer because some may not already know it.**

This prayer should not be the only words we ever speak in prayer. Instead, they should be a model upon which we *base* our prayers and approach the Father. For this session, we'll use the acrostic, **P O W E R** to help us remember the elements of Jesus' model prayer:

Project the acrostic P O W E R on a wall using the "Pray with Power" transparency (Prayer C) or write the acrostic, a letter at a time, on your dry erase or chalk board.

P is for **Praise**. Jesus said God's name was "holy". We should praise God just because he is worthy of our praise.

Practice Pointer:
Jesus said in **Luke 19:40** that if we don't praise him, the "rocks will cry out". God will be praised and it's our privilege to be able to do it.

O is for **Obey**. Jesus asked that God's "will be done on earth as it is in Heaven." His *will* is what He wants to happen. We should pray for

Practice Pointer:
We need to seek God's *face* and not just His *Hand*!

the strength and wisdom to obey God so that we can do His will.

W is for Wrongs. Jesus said to "forgive us our debts as we forgive those who have wronged us". We need to confess our sins to God. God paid for our sins and forgave us when we accepted Jesus as Savior (If we have done so), But we need to ask for forgiveness to keep our lines of communication open with God. Sin blocks that communication - confession opens it back up again.

E is for Entreat. This word simply means to ask for help. To ask God to help us with a math test, or to ask God to help Uncle Bob to get well. Jesus asked God to "give us our daily bread," a basic need for food we all have. Jesus also asked God to, "lead us not into temptation, but deliver us from the evil one." He knew that the power to overcome the devil and to resist temptation came from God. If Jesus needed to spend *hours* in prayer to be victorious, how much more do *we* need to pray? We have the privilege of praying for ourselves and for others.

R is for Remember. We need to remember to thank God for answering our prayers. Paul said, "Don't worry about anything, but pray about everything, and don't forget to *thank* Him for His answers." We need to thank God for prayers He has answered and for being merciful toward us. A true prayer of faith thanks God for an answer even before we realize He has answered it, after all, Jesus said God knows our needs before we ask Him.

Practice Pointer:
This is the only part of the model prayer that Jesus commented on in Matthew. He said we must forgive others if we expect God to forgive us. If we hold grudges, we need to closely examine our relationship with God.

Practice Pointer:
Remember, God is not Santa Claus - where we ask him for *things* but don't try to have a relationship with *Him*. **Matthew 6:33** says God will give us what we need when we seek after Him. Make sure you love God more than the things you ask Him for.

Practice Pointer:
This departs from the model prayer. The scripture reference is **Philippians 4:6** quoted from *The Living Bible*.

Practice Pointer:
James 1:2 says to "consider it pure joy" when troubles come. We should actually be thankful for *problems* because they make us strong.

A Promise to Ponder:
"Let us then approach the throne of grace with confidence, so that we may receive mercy and find grace to help us in our time of need." Hebrews 4:16

Practice Makes Perfect:

Explain to the students that you are going to divide them into teams. The students will stand in a circle and hold hands. Starting with the team leader, they will say a sentence prayer following **only one** of the concepts from the **POWER** acrostic each time they "go around the circle." In other words, the team members will take turns praying one sentence at a time.

Practice Pointer:
Encourage *all* students to pray aloud, but if a person is too shy or uncomfortable, he can squeeze the hand of the next person and that person will pray.

The first sentence prayer should be one that **Praises** God.

**Examples: This sentence prayer may sound something like: "Lord, you are so awesome and I praise you for it."
Or "Father, you are a wonderful God and I worship your name."
Or "God, you are holy and worthy to be praised."**

Practice Pointer:
Often, when we praise God, it's for something He gave us or did for us. But we also need to praise Him just because He is God.

Then the team leader will say one sentence prayer on **obedience**.

Examples: This sentence prayer may sound something like: "God, I need to be nicer to my mom, please help me to do this."

Or "Lord, help me to study my Bible more."
Or "Jesus, I want to honor you with my life today, help me to do your will."

Next will be a sentence prayer on **wrongs.**

Examples: This sentence prayer may sound something like: "God, I have held a grudge against a friend and I need your forgiveness."
Or "Lord, I haven't been acting like I know I should at school lately, please forgive me and help me."
Or "Father, I have had a bad attitude at home and I'm sorry about that."

Practice Pointer:
Be sure to explain to your students that they should **not** confess sins that may hurt others or may not be appropriate in this setting.

Next will be a sentence to **entreat.**

Examples: This sentence prayer may sound something like: "God, please help me to pass that math test tomorrow."
Or "Father, help my friend to stop doing drugs and start living for you."
Or "Lord, help my dad start coming to church."

Practice Pointer:
Remind your students that **James 1:6,7** says we must *believe* God will answer our prayers. If we doubt, we will not get our prayers answered.

The last sentence prayer will be on the word **remember**.

Examples: This sentence prayer may sound something like: "Father, I thank you for my salvation."
Or "God, I thank you for my friends."
Or "Lord Jesus, thank you for getting my parents in church."

Now, divide your students into teams and assign each team a place to go.

Practice Pointer:
Hand out the **Pray with Power** sheets before you divide the students so they can refer to it as they pray.

A Post-Practice Postlude:

Time permitting, have the teams come back to the main assembly room.

Ask: "Did anybody pray aloud for the first time today?"

Tell those students who did how proud you are of them. Get them to discuss their feelings and encourage them that the more they "practice" praying in front of others, the easier it will become.

Encourage the students to take home the hand-out sheet "Pray with Power" (Prayer C) and to discuss this session with their parents and even pray with them, following the **POWER** acrostic.

Have all of your students and workers stand in a circle and join hands. Call on one or more of your new "prayers" to pray, or simply ask for volunteers to pray, saying that when they become silent, you will pray the closing prayer. Dismiss.

> **Practice Pointer:**
> Remember, this model is just that, *a model*. It is meant to help us to pray - but it is not meant to be a formula that you must follow each time you pray. Prayers should be real and from the heart, not a forced formula any more than any other conversation should be.

Prayer A

Cut along the dotted line to make a "prompt instruction" sign: place this sign on the back of a chair near the doorway, with slips of paper with the "prompt" question on them. Make sure pens or pencils are available.

PLEASE TAKE A SLIP OF PAPER AND ANSWER THE QUESTION!

Prayer B

Make enough copies of this page so that each student and worker can get a slip of paper with the "prompt" question on it as they enter the room. Then cut along the dotted lines to make the slips.

Do you believe God has ever answered one of your prayers? If yes, please briefly tell about it:

Do you believe God has ever answered one of your prayers? If yes, please briefly tell about it:

Do you believe God has ever answered one of your prayers? If yes, please briefly tell about it:

Prayer C

Cut along the dotted line, then make enough copies for each student.

PRAY WITH POWER

P is for **Praise**
"Our Father in heaven, Hallowed be your name"
(Matthew 6:9)

O is for **Obey**
"Your will be done on earth as it is in heaven"
(Matthew 6:10)

W is for **Wrongs**
"Forgive us our debts as we also have forgiven our debtors"
(Matthew 6:12)

E is for **Entreat**
"Give us today our daily bread"
(Matthew 6:11)
"...Deliver us from the evil one."
(Matthew 6:13)

R is for **Remember**
"...with thanksgiving, present your requests to God."
(Philippians 4:6)

2

Session Two: **Testimony Practice**

A Peek at the Practice:

By the end of this session, you will have taught your students the importance of being able to say their own testimony in front others and will have led them to practice doing so.

The Primary Objective Points:

Students Will:

- Learn the importance of being able to share their testimony with others.

- Actually practice sharing their testimony in front of their peers.

- Learn how to share their testimony effectively and become more comfortable doing so.

Plan Ahead:

Read through the lesson plan. Personalize it to fit your group's personality. Make any adjustments you deem necessary to fit the size and makeup of your group.

Make copies of the **prompt** question sheets (Test B), then cut them into strips along the dotted line. Make enough strips for each student. Have pens and pencils ready for each student's use.

Make enough copies of the **Sharing Your Testimony** handout sheet (Test C) for each student.

Pray for your students. Think about *your* testimony so you will be prepared to share it in front of your students.

Set a chair by the doorway so students will pass by it as they enter. Place the strips of paper you have prepared on it. Tape the sign **Please take a sheet and answer the question** (Test A), on the chair along with pens or pencils.

Have sheets of paper available for students to write their testimonies on.

Arrange the room so that students can stand in front of the group and share their testimonies. In larger groups, you may want to have space available to divide the students into smaller groups.

Make a transparency of **Sharing Your Testimony**, or have a chalk or dry-erase board available on which to place its elements.

Prompt Your Young People:

> **Practice Pointer:**
> Students do not need to sign their names to their prompt question sheets.

As the students enter the room, they will take a strip of paper and answer the question. Take-up the strips or have a volunteer do so.

Begin your session time as you are most comfortable: Make needed announcements, sing songs, etc.

Next, take prayer requests. Pray, or call on someone to pray -- perhaps someone who demonstrated he was comfortable praying in the last session.

Sort through the "question strips" and read a variety of answers to the students.

> **Practice Pointer:**
> The "prompt" question is fairly lighthearted, so expect some laughter. Try to keep this part of the session as open and fun as is appropriate.

Allow for comments on the answers, including letting students comment on their own answers if they so choose.

Make positive comments on the students' answers on their question strips.

Explain that this is what giving your testimony is - just telling about something that happened to you. This is what we will be talking about in this session:

<u>Sharing your testimony is simply telling about what God has done for you.</u>

Preface the Practice:

Ask: "When you just told about something that happened to you, was it what happened to *you* or someone else?"

Explain that our testimony is about what God has done and is doing in *our* lives. It's not about what God did for someone else - like a bible character or a grandparent (although what happens to our friends and family does affect us). Every testimony is different. God made each of us unique.

Ask: "Do you think your testimony is pretty *boring* and other people have much more interesting testimonies?"

A lot of young people have heard ex-convicts and ex-drug addicts come and share their testimonies. Explain that it is just as much of a miracle for God to save a decent 9-year-old as it is a hardened criminal. You should be proud if you have never lived "in sin" or done drugs. But whether you have or not, God wants all Christians to tell *their* stories to others so they will see that God truly does love everyone and will make anyone's life worth living. God is *most* honored by a person who is saved at an early age and has never stopped loving Him.

Ask: "When we give our testimonies, should we brag about what *we* have done or about what *God* has done in our lives?"

Explain that God should *always* be glorified in what we do and say. A guy in the bible with a very interesting testimony was the apostle Paul. Paul always talked and wrote about what God had done in his life.

Read Acts 26: 4 - 29.

Discuss how Paul was a very religious man, but he persecuted those who followed Christ. But then one day on the road to the city of Damascus, Paul encountered Jesus. Jesus saved him and Paul's life was never the same - now he told everyone he could about Jesus.

When we give our testimonies, we need to follow Paul's basic pattern. There are four basic elements to sharing your testimony.

Practice Pointer:
Paul also gave his testimony in **Acts 22: 1 - 21.** Pieces of his testimony are found throughout his letters and **Acts.**

Project the transparency sheet, "Sharing Your Testimony" on a wall - or write the elements, one at a time, on your chalk or dry-erase board. Go through the elements.

First: Your Life Before Christ.

What was your life like before you became a Christian? It may have been full of sin or troubles - or it may have been young and simple in a Christian home. Did you feel peace and contentment? Were you happy?

Practice Pointer:
Remember that we must tell the truth in our testimonies. Adding to it to make it more interesting is lying and certainly doesn't honor God. At the same time, we need not tell *every* detail either - but only what is appropriate for this setting - and what will not harm others.

Second: How You Became a Christian.

Where were you when you became a Christian? When did you ask Jesus into your heart? How old were you? Was it at church, camp, home, a Bible school? Did your parents help you? A friend? A minister? Tell about the experience.

Third: Your Life Since Christ.

How has becoming a Christian changed your life? Are you happier? Do you have more peace in your life? Has it been harder than before? How do you act differently than before?

Fourth: What God is Doing in Your Life Right Now.

Your testimony should be as fresh as today's newspaper. It should not be just about what God did four years ago, but about how you are growing and what God is doing *today*!

Hand out the sheet, "Sharing Your Testimony" to your students. Hand out the blank sheets of paper and pens or pencils. Ask them to briefly write their testimonies. Explain to them that they need to be able to share their testimonies in less than two minutes.

Give them five to 10 minutes to write their testimonies.

Practice Pointer:
Jesus doesn't save us over a period of time: It is a specific time in a specific setting when we ask Him into our hearts. Youth may not remember the date when they were saved, but they should remember the circumstances (if they were). *If they have not been saved, they don't really have a testimony* - be sensitive: perhaps through this exercise they will see that and want to be saved.

Practice Pointer:
Paul says in **2 Corinthians 5:17** that we *will* be different after we are saved. Not everyone makes dramatic lifestyle changes - but there should be a difference in our lives.

Practice Pointer:
A lot of Christians are "big event oriented". We live from one camp or retreat to another. Help your students see that those events are good, but God wants a relationship with us every day. He should be working in our lives even in the everyday things.

A Promise to Ponder:
"...Then you will be given what to say, for it will not be you speaking, but the Spirit of your Father speaking through you." Matthew 10: 19b -20

Practice Makes Perfect:

Explain to the students that you are going to practice giving your testimonies. <u>The students will come to the front of the room and share their testimonies; they can either read from their sheets - or better, give their testimonies without reading them.</u>

> If you have a larger group, you may want to divide your students into junior high and high school, or by class. You may feel, for instance, your younger students would be too intimidated to stand and speak in front of your high schoolers. If you do divide your students, make sure you have leaders in each group to keep the students on task.

Now, share your testimony with the group. Remember to keep it to two minutes or less. Use the four elements as a guide, but make sure it is in your own thoughts and words.

When you finish, invite the students to come to the front and share their testimonies. (If you divide your students, you may want to do that at this time.) Step away from the podium.

Pray for your students as they speak. Be available to help if they get stuck, but, of course, never ridicule or embarrass your students.
Let the students share until all who wish to have spoken or until time runs out.

> **Practice Pointer:**
> *Silence for a few moments is okay.* None of your students may want to be the first to speak. Eventually, one will speak. If no student will go first, call on a worker or stronger student to do so. If you believe *ahead of time* that no student will go first, you might want to assign a stronger student or worker to go first. Dividing the students may also help.

A Post-Practice Postlude:

If all who wish to have spoken and there is still time, finish the session by complimenting those who shared. Again, never put down your students in any way. You might want to carefully critique your students' testimonies, however:

Again, our testimonies should not be, "look what *I've* done," but, "look what *God* has done in my life." Some students may just want to talk about their friends, or boy and girlfriends. That's because that is the most important thing in their lives right now. Help them see that our testimonies need to be centered around Christ and what *He* has done for us.

As your students become more mature in Christ, they will *want* to talk more and more about Him and what He is doing in their lives.

Time permitting, have all of your students and workers stand in a circle and join hands. (This builds unity.) Pray or call on someone who has shown he is comfortable praying aloud to pray. Dismiss.

Test A

Cut along the dotted line to make a "prompt instruction" sign: Place this sign on the back of a chair near the doorway, with slips of paper with the "prompt" question on them. Make sure pens or pencils are available.

PLEASE TAKE A SLIP OF PAPER AND ANSWER THE QUESTION!

Test B

Make enough copies of this page so that each student and worker can get a slip of paper with the "prompt" question on it as they enter the room. Then cut along the dotted lines to make the slips.

Tell us about a trip or event in your life that was so much fun you will never forget it.

Tell us about a trip or event in your life that was so much fun you will never forget it.

Tell us about a trip or event in your life that was so much fun you will never forget it.

Test C

Cut along the dotted line, then make enough copies for each student and worker.

- -

Sharing Your Testimony

1) Your Life Before Christ.

What was your life like before you became a Christian?

2) How You Became a Christian.

Tell about how Jesus saved you.

3) Your Life Since Christ.

How has becoming a Christian changed you?

4) What God is Doing in Your Life Right Now.

How are you growing? What are you learning? What is happening in your life right now?

3

Session Three: Word Study

A Peek at the Practice:
By the end of this session, you will have taught your students the importance of understanding words and ideas as found in the Bible and will have led the students to practice studying a select group of them.

The Primary Objective Points:

Students Will:

- Learn the importance of taking a word or idea and studying it to better understand it.

- Actually practice studying words in their contexts in the scriptures.

- Become more comfortable working together to discover biblical truth.

Plan Ahead:

Read through the lesson plan. Personalize it to fit your group's personality. Make any adjustments you deem necessary to fit the size and makeup of your group.

Cut along the dotted lines and make copies of the **Bible Term Test** sheet (Word B). Notice that this session's prompt question is a short matching test. Have pens or pencils ready for each student's use.

Make enough copies of the **Words of the Wise** handout sheet (Word C) for each student.

Make copies of the **Team Instruction Sheets** (Word D1 - D5). You will give each team a sheet corresponding to the team numbers. You keep the originals so you can see what each team is doing.

Pray for your students and for the teaching of this session.

Set a chair by the doorway so students will pass by it as they enter. Place the prompt tests on the chair. Tape the sign, **Please take a sheet and follow the Instructions** (Word A), on the back of the chair. Have pens or pencils available.

Be sure you have room available to send the teams into separate rooms or areas.

Either make a transparency, or have a dry-erase board or chalk board available on which to place the elements of **Words of the Wise**.

Prompt Your Young People:

As students enter the room, they will take a piece of paper and take the matching test. Take-up the papers or have a volunteer do so. You will want a volunteer to <u>grade</u> the tests. This should only take a few minutes. You will find the answer key on **Word E.**

Begin your session as you are most comfortable: Make needed announcements, sing songs, etc.

Next, take prayer requests. Pray, or call on someone to pray - perhaps someone who showed he was comfortable praying aloud in the first session.

Sort through the tests. Tell the students, in general, how they did. Don't embarrass or put down the students in any way. Brag on them if they did well.

The idea here is not to make your students feel ignorant, but to show them if they need to work on their basic biblical knowledge - which is an important part of being a disciple.

These are not words we normally use in everyday communication - but they are important because they help explain God's plan for salvation and what He expects from us in return.

Practice Pointer:
Again, it is not necessary for the students to sign their names to this test.

Practice Pointer:
Don't be too discouraged if they do badly. That would just show that they need to learn these concepts.

Practice Pointer:
Be upbeat and positive about teaching these words. An enthusiastic atmosphere will help your students want to learn.

Preface the Practice:

Ask: "So, why do you think it is important for us to understand the 'big words' in the Bible?"

Explain that, again, it is important that we understand the words in the Bible so we can understand what God is saying to us in His love letter to us.

Ask: "Suppose you are a guy and a girl you really liked wrote you a letter and said you were too 'aromatic', and you thought she meant 'amorous' - what difference would that make?

Well, if you are too "amorous", you might be showing too much affection to her in the hall - but if you are too "aromatic", you might need to wear more deodorant! It *is* important that we know what words written to us mean so we can act accordingly.

Ask: "So, if the Bible says we are saved by 'grace' and you think 'grace' is being able to stay up on your in-line skates - why might that be a problem?"

That's why it is important to look at words in their *context* - where they are in the Bible. We don't have to have all the answers or knowledge to be saved or even to grow as Christians, but as we grow, we need that knowledge to help us mature.

> **Practice Pointer:**
> Try not to spend more than about **five minutes** on this element. You will need time for the students to make their presentations.

A Promise to Ponder:
"Call to me and I will answer you and tell you great and unsearchable things you do not know.
Jeremiah 33:3

Practice Makes Perfect:

Explain to your students that you are going to divide them into teams. Be sure to assign each team a place to go *before* they divide into teams. Give each team its **team instruction sheet**. Have each team elect a spokesperson who will also be the leader on that team. Tell the students to read the instructions on their sheet and follow them. They will then come back and report to the rest of the group.

Practice Pointer:
You can divide your students into teams by "counting off" **one through five**, or by rows or seating.

Now, divide your students into five teams. If you have five or less students, consider giving each student an instruction strip. Each student would then be a "team".

Give the teams about **10 minutes** to prepare for their presentations, once they divide.

Practice Pointer:
Be sure to tell the teams how much time they have to prepare their presentations *before* they divide.

The teams will now come back together and make their reports. Have the teams make their reports in order, corresponding to their team numbers on the **team instruction sheets**.

> **Practice Pointer:**
> The teams will each need **five to 10 minutes** to make their reports. You will need about **10 minutes** for the **Postlude.** Be sure to allot **35 to 40 minutes** *after* the teams return.

A Post-Practice Postlude:

Hand out the **Words of the Wise** sheet (Word C).
Use the transparency or write the words on a chalk or dry-erase board. Go over each word and help the students understand them. Try not to repeat what the students have already said, but quickly go over each word and its meaning.

Encourage the students to take the **Words of the Wise** sheets home to show their parents.

Pray. Dismiss.

> **Practice Pointer:**
> Be sure to brag on each team for its effort and presentation.

Word A

Cut along the dotted line to make a "prompt instruction" sign: place this sign on the back of a chair near the doorway, with the "prompt tests" on it. Make sure pens or pencils are available.

PLEASE TAKE A SHEET OF PAPER AND FOLLOW THE INSTRUCTIONS

Word B

Cut along the dotted line, then make enough copies of this test for each student. Place it on a chair and set it near the doorway. Make sure pens or pencils are available.

Bible Word Test

Please match each Bible word with its best definition:

___ 1) Faith
___ 2) Grace
___ 3) Holiness
___ 4) Justification
___ 5) Reconciliation
___ 6) Redemption
___ 7) Repentance
___ 8) Righteousness
___ 9) Salvation
___ 10) Sin

A. Declared guilt-free; "just if I'd never sinned."
B. Enemies being made friends again.
C. To buy back.
D. Missing the mark.
E. Believing in something - even when you cannot see it.
F. To be set apart. Also, The essence of God.
G. To feel sorry for actions and turn away from sins.
H. Unearned favor or kindness.
I. Being morally upright.
J. To be delivered from some danger or evil.

40

Word C

Cut along the dotted line, then make enough copies for each student and worker.

Words of the Wise

1) **Faith**
   Believing in something - even when you cannot see it. **Hebrews 11:1**
2) **Grace**
   Unearned favor or kindness. Great Riches At Christ's Expense. **Ephesians 2:8,9**
3) **Holiness**
   To be set apart. The essence of God. What God *is* and what He demands that we be. To be *sanctified* means to be made holy. Our moral standards must be *different* and *above* the world's. **1 Peter 1:16**
4) **Justification**
   Declared not guilty. "*Just if I'd* never sinned". We *are* guilty of sin, but when God *justifies* us, through Christ, He declares us, "not guilty". **Titus 3:7**
5) **Reconciliation**
   Enemies being made friends again. Sin makes us "enemies" with God, but we become his friends again when we accept Jesus as savior. **Romans 5:10,11**
6) **Redemption**
   To buy back. To redeem something is to purchase or trade for it. Jesus *bought* us with his blood. **Ephesians 1:7**
7) **Repentance**
   To feel sorry for actions and turn away from sins. It means to turn and go the complete other direction from where you were going. **Luke 5: 31,32**
8) **Righteousness**
   Being morally upright. Jesus *is* our righteousness. **Romans 3:21,22**
9) **Salvation**
   To be delivered from some danger or evil. Jesus is the *only* way to the Father. **Acts 4:12**
10) **Sin**
    Missing the mark. Falling short of the nature and character of God. **1 John 1:8,9,10**

Word D1
Team Instruction Sheet

Make a copy of this sheet then cut along the dotted line.
Give each team its instruction sheet.

- -

Team 1

Select a spokesperson for your team. Your team is going to report to the main assembly what the words **Faith** and **Redemption** mean.

Please read and prepare to answer the questions below in front of the group:

FAITH

Look up **Hebrews 11:1**. Have a team member read it aloud. What, according to this passage, does the word **faith** mean? _____
_____

Now, in your own words, what is **faith**? _____
_____

Read **Hebrews 11: 1 - 38**. What was it all those Old Testament people had that enabled them to do what God wanted them to do? _____

Read **Hebrews 11:6**. It is impossible to please God without what? _____
Why do you think that is? _____

REDEMPTION

Look up **Leviticus 25: 47 - 49**. What are these verses saying? _____
_____
_____

So, what does the word **Redeem** mean? _____
_____

Read **Ephesians 1:7**. If **Redemption** is the forgiveness of our sins by the blood of Christ, does that mean he *bought* us? _____. If yes, what was the price? _____. Was that an *expensive* or *cheap* price? _____. If expensive, what does that say about how valuable we are in Christ? _____.
If Jesus *bought* us, does that mean he *owns* us? _____. If yes, then what do we owe him in return? _____

Word D2
Team Instruction Sheet

Make a copy of this sheet then cut along the dotted line.
Give each team its instruction sheet.

Team 2

Select a spokesperson for your team. Your team is going to report to the main assembly what the words **Grace** and **Repentance** mean.

Please read and prepare to answer the questions below in front of the group:

GRACE

Look up **Ephesians 2:1 - 9**. Have a team member read it aloud. Paul says twice, "It is by _____ you have been saved." He says we are saved by **grace** and not by _____.
What, in your own words, does **grace** mean? _____

According to this passage, is **grace** something we can *earn*? _____ . Why does God give us such kindness? _____
_____ What should our response to God's **grace** be? _____

REPENTANCE

Look up **Luke 5: 31, 32**. Have a team member read it aloud. Who does Jesus say needs a doctor, the healthy or the sick? _____ . Spiritually, what is he saying? _____

Read **Acts 3:19**. What did Peter say would happen if you **repented** and turned to God? _____

Read **Matthew 4:17**. What was it Jesus preached? _____

Read **Matthew 27:3**. The NIV Bible says Judas was "seized with remorse", the King James Bible says, "he **repented**". So based on these scriptures, what does **repentance** mean?

Why does God want us to **repent** of our sins ? _____

Word D3
Team Instruction Sheet

Make a copy of this sheet then cut along the dotted line.
Give each team its instruction sheet.

Team 3

Select a spokesperson for your team. Your team is going to report to the main assembly what the words **Holiness** and **Righteousness** mean.

Please read and prepare to answer the questions below in front of the group:

HOLINESS

Look up **1 Peter 1: 13 - 16**. Have a team member read it aloud. What <u>three</u> things does Peter say to do in verse **13**? _____
_____
_____

What does he say to *not to do* in verse **14**? _____
_____

What does he say to be in verses **15** and **16**? _____. Why does he say we should be that? _____
Now read **1 Peter 2:9**. What <u>four</u> things does Peter say Christians are? _____
_____
_____

What, in your own words, does **Holiness** mean? _____
_____

RIGHTEOUSNESS

Look up **Romans 3: 21 - 22**. What is Paul saying has been made known? _____
_____. In verse **22**, where does he say this **righteousness** comes from? _____
Look up **1 John 1:9**. What is it God will purify us from? _____
read **1 John 2:1**. What does John call Jesus? _____
Look up **Ephesians 6:14**. Read it aloud. Paul says to put on the breastplate of what? _____
_____. Find **Romans 6:16**. Paul says *obedience* leads to what? _____
What, in your own words, does **righteousness** mean? _____

Word D4
Team Instruction Sheet

Make a copy of this sheet then cut along the dotted line.
Give each team its instruction sheet.

Team 4

Select a spokesperson for your team. Your team is going to report to the main assembly what the words **Justification** and **Salvation** mean.

Please read and prepare to answer the questions below in front of the group:

JUSTIFICATION

Look up **Romans 3:28**. Have a team member read it aloud. According to this verse, how is a person **justified**? _____. Read **Romans 5: 9**. How, in this verse, are we **justified**? _____. Who, then, paid the price for us to be **justified**? _____. How did he pay that price? _____
_____. Read **Titus 3:7**. How, according to this verse, are we **justified**? _____. What do we have hope of, since we have been **justified**? _____. What, in your own words, does **justification** mean?
_____
Who, according to the above verses, is **justified** _____
Does this mean our sins are forgiven? _____

SALVATION

Look up **Acts 4:12**. Read it aloud. *Who* is **salvation** found in? _____. What do you think this verse is saying a person is **saved** from? _____. Read **John 3: 16, 17**. Why does verse 17 say Jesus came into the world? _____
_____. How is a person **saved** from death, according to verse 16? _____
_____. Read **Ephesians 2:8,9**. How is a person **saved**, according to these verses? _____. In verse **9**, how is a person *not* **saved**? _____. Read **John 14:6**. Who did Jesus say is the only way to the Father? _____. What else is a person **saved** from, when he accepts Christ, according to **Romans 6: 22** ("set free" from)? _____
Then, according to that verse, what is the result? _____.

45

Word D5
Team Instruction Sheet

Make a copy of this sheet then cut along the dotted line.
Give each team its instruction sheet.

Team 5

Select a spokesperson for your team. Your team is going to report to the main assembly what the words **Reconciliation** and **Sin** mean.

Please read and prepare to answer the questions below in front of the group:

RECONCILIATION

Look up **Romans 5: 9 - 11**. Have a team member read it aloud. What, according to verse 10, were we to God, before He saved us? _____. Read verse 11. In *whom* have we now received **reconciliation**? _____. So, are Christians still God's enemies? _____. How, in verse 10, were we **reconciled** to God? _____. Read **2 Corinthians 5: 17 - 21**. In verse 19, it says, because God **reconciled** Christians through Christ, he doesn't count our what? _____. In verse 21, it says God made Jesus to be _____ so that in him, we might become the _____
So God is exchanging our what for Jesus' what? _____
What, in your own words, does **reconciliation** mean? _____

SIN

Look up **1 John 1: 8 - 1 John 2:2**. Have a team member read it aloud. What is it John is saying everyone does? _____. If we confess that **sin**, what, in verse 9, will God do? _____. In verse 2:2, who does the Bible say will defend us if we **sin**? _____. Read **Romans 3:23**. Who does Paul say have **sinned** and fallen short of God's glory? _____. Read **John 8:2 - 11**. In verse 11, Jesus tells the woman to leave her life of what? _____. Read **1 John 3: 4 - 10**. Verse 4 says those who **sin** break the law. What law? _____. Verse 6 says no one who lives in God keeps on what? _____. Verse 8 says those who do "what is **sinful**" are of whom? _____. What do you think John means by "keeps on **sinning**" and "continues to **sin**"? _____. Do you think a Christian will ever **sin**? Discuss _____.

Word E

Bible Word Test - Key

- __E__ 1) Faith
- __H__ 2) Grace
- __F__ 3) Holiness
- __A__ 4) Justification
- __B__ 5) Reconciliation
- __C__ 6) Redemption
- __G__ 7) Repentance
- __I__ 8) Righteousness
- __J__ 9) Salvation
- __D__ 10) Sin

4

Session Four: **Scripture Memory Practice**

A Peek at the Practice:
By the end of this session, you will have taught your students the importance of memorizing scripture and will have led them to actually memorize one or more verses that begin with the letters of the alphabet.

The Primary Objective Points:

Students Will:

- Learn the importance of memorizing scripture.

- Actually practice memorizing selected scriptures.

- Become more comfortable memorizing the scripture.

Plan Ahead:

Read through the lesson plan. Personalize it to fit your group's personality. Make any adjustments you deem necessary to fit the size and makeup of your group.

Make copies of the **prompt** question sheets (Script B), then cut them into strips along the dotted lines. Make enough strips for each student. Have pens or pencils available for each student's use.

Make copies of the **Alphabet Scriptures** team sheets (Script C1 - C5). *You will need five sheets per team.* <u>You will also need to make enough copies of these verses to give *each* student all 26 verses as a take-home packet.</u>

Pray for your students and the teaching of this session. Memorize as many scriptures found in this session as you can.

Set a chair by the doorway so students will pass by it as they enter. Place the **prompt question strips** on the chair. Tape the sign, **"Please take a sheet and answer the question"** (Script A), on the back of the chair.

Be sure you have room available to divide the students into teams as you did in the last session.

Practice Pointer:
Please notice that you will be making lots of copies for this session. Copy the **Alphabet Scriptures** team sheets, then staple them together to give each student as he leaves so he can memorize a scripture for each letter of the alphabet.

Prompt Your Young People:

As the students enter the room, each will take a **prompt question strip** and answer the question. Take up the strips or have a volunteer do so.

Begin your session time as you are most comfortable: Make needed announcements, sing songs, etc.

Next, take prayer requests. Pray, or call on someone to pray - perhaps someone who showed he is comfortable praying aloud in the first session.

Sort through the **question strips** and read a variety of answers to the students. Give positive comments on why the students like particular scriptures. Let them comment on their answers if they so choose.

The idea of the prompt question is to help the students think about how many scriptures they know, if any at all.

You want to encourage them to memorize as many verses as they possibly can. The "alphabet scriptures" idea is just to make it more interesting for them to memorize 26 different verses.

They *can* memorize that many scriptures and will feel very good about themselves for doing so - don't sell them short.

> **Practice Pointer:**
> Again, students do not need to sign their names to their **question strips**.

> **Practice Pointer:**
> What you may find is that some students cannot write *a single* scripture. Some students know lots of verses and some only a few. The idea of this session is to teach them that they need to continue to memorize the word. Don't discourage them if they don't know any - just encourage them to get started!

Preface the Practice:

Ask: "Suppose the American army, when it went to Germany to fight in World War Two, didn't take any weapons. No guns, tanks, bullets, bombs - nothing. Would they have done any good, fighting the Nazis with their *bare fists!?*"

Dumb question, right? But isn't that just what Christians are doing if we are fighting the enemy without the "Sword of the Spirit?" Explain that when a person becomes a Christian, he is in a spiritual war whether he likes it or not. Many Christians live defeated lives because they are beaten by the enemy on a daily basis. We need our armor on for protection, and we need to *fight back*.

Practice Pointer:
The *enemy* we are fighting against is the "spiritual forces of evil in the heavenly realms" mentioned in **Ephesians 6:12**.

Have a volunteer read **Ephesians 6:10 - 17**.

Ask: "What is the only *offensive weapon* mentioned in the *'armor of God?'*"

Explain that the *sword of the spirit, which is the word of God* is listed as our only offense against the enemy. So, we are fighting an enemy without a weapon if we don't have any scripture memorized!

Have a volunteer read **Matthew 4: 1 - 11**.

Ask: "The devil tempts Jesus in this passage three times. How does Jesus answer him each time?"

Explain that Jesus fought the temptation of the devil with scripture. If *Jesus* needed to know the scripture to fight temptation, don't we need it much more?

Have a volunteer read **Psalm 119:11**.

Ask: "Why did the writer of this Psalm say he wanted to hide God's word in his heart?"

Explain that the writer wanted to have God's word - his law and the Scripture - "in his heart" so that he wouldn't sin. "In his heart" would mean he knew God's word. We say that we know something "by heart" - which means we have memorized it. The Psalmist meant more than just "head knowledge" though, he also meant he believed it and it was important to him.

Practice Pointer:
The only scripture written when Jesus came was the Old Testament. Jesus obviously knew it well - and had memorized many scriptures. The devil also used scripture to *tempt* Jesus, so Jesus had to know the scripture well to counter his attack.

Practice Pointer:
The word of God can mean Jesus himself and also the spoken and written *words* of God - The Bible.

A Promise to Ponder:
"For the word of God is living and active. Sharper than any double-edged sword, it penetrates even to dividing soul and spirit, joints and marrow; it judges the thoughts and attitudes of the heart." **Hebrews 4:12**

Practice Makes Perfect:

Explain to the students that you are going to divide them into **five** teams. Each team will memorize **five** scriptures (team five will have to memorize six). They can do this by having the whole team memorize all five scriptures or by having each team member memorize one or more passage.

> **Practice Pointer:**
> They *do* need to memorize the address (book, chapter, verse) of the scripture - this is part of understanding the Bible in context.

> I recommend having each team member memorize all five (or six) verses. Some students may not be able to memorize that many, but most can.

You will give them their **Alphabet Scriptures** team sheets when you divide them.

Give the teams only about **20 minutes** once they divide to memorize their scriptures.

Explain that they will then come back together and present the scriptures in order. Have the teams stand together and quote their scriptures together - or each team member can quote a scripture. They will be quoting a scripture beginning with each letter of the alphabet.

> **Practice Pointer:**
> Okay, we had to *fudge* a little on **x**! The verses are all in either the *King James Version, New King James Version* or *The New International Version*.

Go over the **memorization tips** on the next page before you divide the students into teams.

Before you divide them into teams, go over these guidelines to help them memorize and retain the passages:

- Look for rhymes or meter (rhythm) in the verses - if you can sing it you can easily remember it. (If your students can come back and "sing" the verse, or maybe say it while they use "hand motions," they will probably never forget it.)

- Memorize only a phrase at a time - don't try to "bite off" all of longer verses at once.

- Make sure you understand the passage. You will never remember it if you don't know what it's talking about.

- Make sure you understand all of the *words* in the passage so you can fully understand what it is saying.

- Notice the *address* of the scripture. It is important to learn scripture in its *context*.

- Try to make number associations to memorize the addresses.
  (For instance: For Psalm 37:4 -- 3 From 7 is 4.)

A Post-Practice Postlude:

After the teams have quoted their scriptures, be sure to brag on them and how well they did.

Give each student *all* of the **Alphabet Scriptures** team sheets (Script C1 - C5) so they can take them home. Encourage each student to memorize the rest of the scriptures so they will know a scripture for each letter of the alphabet.

Explain to the students that they will have to *use* these scriptures to be able to retain them. They will need to quote them to each other and to their friends and families on a regular basis or they will forget the verses.

You might want to tell the students you will reward them in some way (free pizza at the next pizza party, a discount on a T-shirt, free candy, etc.) if they can quote all of the "alphabet scriptures" for you when you meet again.

Practice Pointer:
The reason this is important is because students need some *accountability* to encourage them to accomplish something like memorizing this many scriptures.

Have the students stand and join hands. Pray or call on someone to pray. Dismiss.

Script A

Cut along the dotted line to make a "prompt instruction sign:
Place this sign on the back of a chair near the doorway, with
the prompt question slips on it. Make sure pens and pencils are
available.

PLEASE TAKE A SLIP OF PAPER AND ANSWER THE QUESTION!

Script B

Make enough copies of this page so that each student can get a slip of paper with the "prompt" question on it as he enters the room. Cut along the dotted lines to make the strips.

Please write your favorite Bible Verse, by memory, then briefly tell why you like this verse.

Please write your favorite Bible Verse, by memory, then briefly tell why you like this verse.

Please write your favorite Bible Verse, by memory, then briefly tell why you like this verse.

Script C1

Cut along the dotted line and make enough copies so that each team will have **five** copies (six for team five) and also so that each student will have a complete set of all 26 (A - Z) Scriptures.

Team 1

A   "Ask and it will be given to you, seek and you will find, knock and the door will be opened to you."

Luke 11:9

B   "But they that wait upon the Lord shall renew their strength; they shall mount with wings as eagles; they shall run and not be weary; and they shall walk and not faint."

Isaiah 40:31

C   "Cast all your care on him, for he cares for you."

1 Peter 5:7

D   "Delight yourself in the Lord and he will give you the desires of your heart."

Psalm 37:4

E   "Enter through the narrow gate. For wide is the gate and broad is the road that leads to destruction and many enter through it."

Matthew 7:13

Script C2

Team 2

F "For God so loved the world that he gave his one and only son, that whoever believes in him shall not perish but have eternal life." **John 3:16**

G "Go therefore and make disciples of all nations, baptizing them in the name of the Father and of the Son and of the Holy Spirit." **Matthew 28:19**

H "Honor your father and your mother, so that you may live long in the land the Lord your God is giving you." **Exodus 20:12**

I "I am the way and the truth and the life. No one comes to the Father except through me." **John 14:6**

J "Judge not that you be not judged." **Matthew 7:1**

Script C3

Team 3

K "Know that the Lord has set apart the Godly for himself; the Lord will hear when I call him."
           Psalm 4:3

L "Love is patient, love is kind. It does not envy, it does not boast it is not proud."
           1 Corinthians 13:4

M "My soul finds rest in God alone; my salvation comes from him."
           Psalm 62:1

N "Not by might nor by power, but by my Spirit says the Lord Almighty."
           Zechariah 4:6

O "O Lord, our Lord, how majestic is your name in all the earth!"
           Psalm 8:9

Script C4

Team 4

P "Put on the whole armor of God so that you can take your stand against the devil's schemes."
Ephesians 6:11

Q "Quick! Bring the best robe and put it on him. Put a ring on his finger and sandals on his feet."
Luke 15:22

R "Rejoice in the Lord always. Again I will say, rejoice!"
Philippians 4:4

S "Submit yourselves then to God. Resist the devil, and he will flee from you."
James 4:7

T "The thief comes only to steal and kill and destroy; I have come that they may have life, and have it to the full."
John 10:10

Script C5

Team 5

U "Unless the Lord builds the house, its builders labor in vain; unless the Lord watches over the city, the watchmen stand guard in vain."
Psalm 127:1

V "Verily, verily, I say unto thee, except a man be born again, he cannot see the kingdom of God."
John 3:3

W "Whoever calls on the name of the Lord shall be saved."
Romans 10:13

X "Examine me, O Lord, and prove me; Try my mind and my heart."
Psalm 26:2

Y "Yet in all these things, we are more than conquerors through Him who loved us."
Romans 8:37

Z "Zeal for your house consumes me."
Psalm 69:9

5

Session Five: Worship Practice

A Peek at the Practice:
By the end of this session, you will have taught your students the importance of true worship and will have led them to practice worshiping God.

The Primary Objective Points:

Students Will:

- Learn the importance of true worship.

- Study Biblical characters who demonstrated true worship.

- Actually practice worshiping God as a group.

Practice Pointer:
You may be wondering if all of your students will want to go into one or two of the teams and ignore the others. We recently had about 10 go into drama and only one went into speech. But it worked fine. Let the students go where they choose. You might, however, want to steer students who really don't seem to know where to go into teams that might provide a good balance.

Plan Ahead:

Read through the lesson plan. Personalize it to fit your group's personality. Make any adjustments you deem necessary to fit the size and makeup of your group.

You will need a small amount of preparation *in advance* to make this session work properly. You are going to let your students choose from five teams in which to participate. Each team will need some **supplies**, which you will need to secure in advance, as follows:

Team 1, the **music** team, will provide music for the rest of the group. It would be very helpful if you **announce before hand** that any students who might want to be on this team to bring their musical instruments (guitars, flutes, etc.), or to bring accompaniment tapes. You can provide a **hymnal** or other **song books**.

Team 2, the **art** team, will need some **art supplies.** You will need to supply poster boards and markers, modeling clay, like "play dough", pencils, or even paint and brushes if you so choose.

Team 3, the **poetry and prose** team, will need pens or pencils and paper.

Team 4, the **acting** team, will need pens or pencils and paper.

Team 5, the **speech** team, will need pens and pencils and paper.

All of the teams will need access to a **Bible**.

Make copies of the **prompt** question sheets (Worship B), then cut them into strips along the dotted lines. Make enough strips for each student. Have pens or pencils ready for each student's use.

Make enough copies of the **Who, What and Why of Worship** handout sheet (Worship C) for each student.

Make a copy of each **worship team** sheet (Worship D1 - D4). Place them in the room which you have assigned to that team.

Make a copy of the **worship team door signs** (Worship E1 - E5) on colorful paper. Place the signs on room doors (or areas) to designate where each team will meet.

Pray for your students and for this session. Begin to examine *your* worship practices and attitudes so that you will be ready to lead by example.

Set a chair by the doorway so students will pass by it as they enter. Place the **prompt** question strips on it. Tape the sign "Please take a sheet and answer the question" (Worship A) on the back of the chair.

Prompt Your Young People:

As the students enter the room, they will take a **prompt** question strip and answer the question. Take up the strips or have a volunteer do so.

Begin your session time as you are most comfortable: Make needed announcements, sing songs, etc.

> **Practice Pointer:**
> I highly recommend singing with your students. This is a great way to *worship* together with them. You can play an instrument, use tapes or find someone to help you. Let your students lead in the singing as much as possible. To conserve time for *this* session, you may want to **save the singing** for the *music team* which will lead in musical worship later in the session.

Next, take prayer requests. Pray, or call on someone to pray.

Sort through the **prompt** question strips and read a variety of answers to the students. Again, never criticize the students' answers.

Allow for comments on the answers.

Brag on your students for the creativity in their answers. Help them see that **worship** is more than just sitting in church singing.

Preface the Practice:

Ask: "So, what is *worship* anyway?"

Explain that the word **worship** means "worth-ship" in the English language. In the Hebrew and Greek languages, it meant "to bow down" - or to lie prostrate on the ground before something. It means to give honor and respect to something, to declare the "worth" of someone or something.

Ask: "If that is the case, then what is God worth to you?"

The Bible declares that God and God alone is worthy of all praise, glory, honor, power and of our very lives.

The Bible also says we are to love God with all of our hearts, souls and minds. God said He must be first in our lives and that we must put "no other gods" before Him.

Simply put, God must be the most important thing in our lives.

Ask: "Okay, so how do we worship God?"

The students have already given some ways in their **prompt** question strips. Explain that God is more interested in our *hearts and attitudes* than anything we do outwardly. We can sit in church and sing, but not really worship.

Practice Pointer:
Please watch your time during this element. You will need to save 20 minutes for the teams to prepare, then 30 to 40 more for their presentations. If you use all of the material in this session, you will need about an hour and a half to present it.

Practice Pointer:
Revelation 4:11, Revelation 22:8,9, Hebrews 13:15, Romans 12:1.

Practice Pointer:
Matthew 22:37, Exodus 20:3.

Practice Pointer:
Hosea 6:6 says, "I don't want your sacrifices, I want your love. I don't want your offerings, I want you to know me." (TLB)

Worship is acknowledging with your mind that God is perfect and holy, then *doing something about it* to show your love and respect for Him. That might mean telling Him privately that you praise Him, or it might mean giving your best to Him in some form of public address.

Have someone read Romans 12:1

Paul talks about our "act of worship" in this verse. He says that is "offering our bodies as living sacrifices, holy and pleasing to God."

Ask: "What does Paul mean by 'living sacrifices'?"

Explain that God wants us to *live for Him* - to think about Him before we make every decision, to talk to Him daily, to live in such a way that we *honor* Him with our lives. To spend our time, money and energy in a way that is pleasing to Him. Sometimes, this may involve some *sacrifice*, but that is proof that our devotion is real.

The writer of Hebrews said to "continually offer to God a sacrifice of praise - the fruit of lips that confess his name."
Another sacrifice that God wants from us is for us to praise Him. The Bible says He will be praised - so it is our privilege to do it.

You might think of a "sacrifice of praise" as praising God whether we feel like or not.

Have someone read Job 1:20- 21.

Explain that Job **worshiped** God on the worst day

Practice Pointer:
Sacrifice has always been associated with **worship**. In the Old Testament, animals were sacrificed to atone for sins. Jesus himself was sacrificed for our sins. Now, in return, we are to offer a *living* sacrifice back to God.

Practice Pointer:
Luke 19:40 says if we don't worship God the "rocks will cry out."

of his life. Why? Because, he knew that even if he didn't understand everything, God was God and deserved his worship and devotion.

The Bible is full of people who worshiped God when they saw his love and power. **Daniel, Moses, Mary** are just a few examples. The Bible teaches that we need to worship God all the time - when times are good and when they are the pits.

Practice Pointer:
Daniel 2:19 - 23
Exodus 15:1 - 18
Luke 1:46 - 55

Ask: "Do you think everybody worships something?"

Explain that God created us with a natural desire to worship something. He created us that way so we would seek *Him*, but most people worship something or someone else. Of course, nothing else will satisfy that longing except worshiping God himself.

Practice Pointer:
People worship everything from sports and sports heroes, to friends, to celebrities, to material things, to hobbies, to popularity.

As we mentioned earlier, the very first commandment of the **Ten Commandments** is that we put no other gods before God. The second is not to make an idol to worship.

Practice Pointer:
Exodus 20:3 - 4

Have someone read Matthew 6:19 - 24.

Jesus says we will serve either God or money - but not both. You can tell what a person <u>worships</u> by what he talks about the most, spends his time and money on and gets the most excited about. In other words, what he "treasures". (Verse 21)

A Promise to Ponder:
"Yet a time is coming and has now come when the true worshipers will worship the Father in spirit and truth, for they are the kind of worshipers the Father seeks." **John 4:23**

Practice Makes Perfect:

Explain to the students that, at this time, they will choose a worship team and go into that team's room or area. Explain that each team will lead the rest of the group in worship according to its instructions.

Each team will have **20 minutes** to prepare its presentation, then **four to seven minutes** to lead in worship (through its presentation) in front of the rest of the students in the main assembly.

Practice Pointer:
You will need to keep things moving during this time. They will need all of their team time to prepare their presentations. Go around and make sure they are staying on task. You will need to keep things moving during the presentations as well.

Point out to the students before you dismiss them into their teams that in true **worship**, *we* are the performers and *God* is the audience. Some people think *they* are the audience and the worship leaders on stage are the performers. Again, true worship is in our *hearts*; the performance is just an outward sign.

Now, dismiss the students into the teams of their choosing - and tell them to come back together in 20 minutes to make their presentations.

A Post-Practice Postlude:

As in every session, compliment the students for their presentation. Tell them how proud you are of the work they put into their presentations.

Hand out the **Who, What and Why of Worship** handout sheets (Worship C). Encourage them to take them home and discuss them and this session with their parents.

Have your students stand in a circle and join hands.
Pray or call on someone to pray.
Dismiss.

Worship A

Cut along the dotted line to make a **prompt** instruction sign. Place this sign on the back of a chair near the doorway, with the **prompt** question strips on it. Make sure pens or pencils are available.

PLEASE TAKE A SLIP OF PAPER AND ANSWER THE QUESTION

Worship B

Make enough copies of the page so that each student
can get a **prompt** question strip as they enter the room.
Cut along the dotted lines to make the strips.

How many ways can you name in which a person can express worship to God?

How many ways can you name in which a person can express worship to God?

How many ways can you name in which a person can express worship to God?

Worship C

Cut along the dotted line, then make enough copies for each student.

The **Who, What** and **Why** of
Worship

Who?

Everyone worships *something!* God says we must worship Him and Him alone.
Exodus 20:3
Jesus says we will either serve God or money - but not both. We must choose.
Matthew 6:24

What?

What is worship? In Hebrew and Greek, it means to "bow down to". In the English language, it means to express what something is "worth" to you. God wants us to love Him with all of our hearts, souls, and minds. In other words, He must be the most important thing in our lives. We express that in many ways, both publicly and privately. God is always the audience and we are the performers. Obviously, we want to give our best to God. Paul says our act of worship is to give God a "living sacrifice" of our bodies to God which is something we do every day. Hebrews says to offer a "sacrifice of praise".
Romans 12:1
Hebrews 13:15

Why?

Job worshiped God on the *worst* day of his life.
Job 1:21
Mary worshiped God on one of the *best* days of her life.
Luke 1:46 - 55
We don't just worship God for when we think He is being good to us, we worship Him all the time *because of who he is*. God is worthy of our praise (**Hebrews 13:15**) and all glory, honor and power (**Revelation 4:11**).
If we don't worship God, "the stones will cry out" to do so. It is our honor and privilege to worship the awesome God of the universe.

Worship D1

Cut along the dotted line. Make two copies of each team instruction sheet. One for you and one for each team.

TEAM 1   MUSIC

Elect a leader for your team.

Find a way to worship God using **Music**. Everyone needs to participate.

You will lead the rest of the group in worship through music when all of the students get back together.
You can sing, play instruments, do a drama (with no words spoken) or pantomime to a song, or some combination of all of these.

You will have **4 to 7 minutes** to make your presentation to the main assembly when you get back together.

TEAM 2   ART

Elect a leader for your team.

Find a way to worship God using **Art**. Everyone needs to participate.

You may draw a picture depicting how you feel about God or that depicts some scene from the Bible.
You may make a sculpture with the modeling clay that depicts a scene or story from the Bible or an issue that modern teenagers face.

You will have **4 to 7 minutes** to make a presentation to the rest of the group.

Worship D2

TEAM 3   *POETRY AND PROSE*

Elect a leader for your team.

Find a way to worship God using **Poetry or Prose**.

You will lead the rest of the group in worship by presenting a poem or story you will write. Everyone needs to participate.
You might want to re-write a Bible story using clean modern "street" language.
You might want to write a poem about how you feel about God.
Or both.
(Some good Bible stories that you might want to use are found in: John 3, John 8:1 - 11, John 9, John 21, Luke 8:40 - 56, Luke 10:30 - 37, and Luke 15:11 - 32)

You will have **4 to 7 minutes** to make your presentation to the rest of the group.

Worship D3

TEAM 4   **DRAMA**

Elect a leader for your team.

Find a way to worship God using **Acting**.

You may write a skit or drama based on a Bible Story or one that depicts modern teenagers dealing with spiritual issues. Everyone needs to participate.

(Some good Bible stories that you might want to use are found in Matthew 18:21 - 35, Luke 15:11 - 32, Luke 10:30 - 37, and Luke 8:4 - 15.)

You will have **4 to 7 minutes** to make your presentation to the rest of the group.

Worship D4

TEAM 5   SPEECH

Elect a leader for your team.

Find a way to worship God through the **spoken word.**

Decide on an order and what each person will do. Plan for each person to say a word of worship to God.

> One or more may want to pray.
> One or more may want to quote a scripture.
> One or more may want to give his or her testimony.
> One or more may want to give God a "praise offering", telling
> why God is worthy of praise and our worship.

You will have from **4 to 7 minutes** to make your total presentation to the rest of the group, so please guage your time carefully.

Worship E1

Cut along the dotted lines. Make a copy of each sign on a colorful sheet of paper. Tape the signs to designate the rooms or area where each team will meet.

WORSHIP
in
MUSIC

Worship E2

WORSHIP THROUGH ART

Worship E3

POETRY & PROSE

Worship E4

WORSHIP THROUGH DRAMA

Worship E5

WORSHIP THROUGH SPEECH

6

Session Six: **Bible Study Practice**

_____

_____

A Peek at the Practice:
By the end of this session, you will have taught your students to study the Bible in context, a chapter at a time, and make a presentation on what they have learned.

The Primary Objective Points:

Students Will:

- Learn the importance of Bible study.

- Work together to study a chapter of the Bible.

- Make presentations of what they have learned.

Plan Ahead:

Read through the lesson plan. Personalize it to fit your group's personality. Make any adjustments you deem necessary to fit the size and makeup of your group.

You will divide the students into **four** teams, and each team will need access to a Bible. Make sure you have space available to send the teams into separate rooms or areas.

Make copies of the **prompt** question sheets (Bible B), then cut them into strips along the dotted lines. Make enough strips for each student. Have pens or pencils ready for each student's use.

Pick which chapter you wish to study (Bible C1 or Bible C2). Make copies of the **Bible study team sheets**, either C1 or C2. You will need a **team sheet** for each of the **four** teams. Place a team sheet in the room or area where each team will meet.

Make enough copies of **God's Amazing Love Letter** (Bible D) for each student.

Pray for your students and for this session. Study the chapter you choose (Bible C1 or C2) so you will be familiar with it.

Set a chair by the doorway so students will pass by it as they enter. Place the **prompt** question strips on it. Tape the sign "Please take a sheet and answer the question" (Bible A) on the back of the chair. Make sure pens or pencils are available.

Practice Pointer:
Encourage your students to bring their Bibles to church and to Bible studies. The Bible studies in this session are based on the New International Version of the Bible.

Prompt Your Young People:

As the students enter the room, they will take a **prompt** question strip and answer the question. Take up the strips or have a volunteer do so.

Begin your session as you are most comfortable: Make needed announcements, sing songs, etc.

Next, take prayer requests. Pray or call on someone to pray.

Sort through the **prompt** question strips and read a variety of answers to the students. Always be careful not to criticize the students' answers.

Allow for comments on the answers.

Brag on your students for having a favorite book of the Bible and for their reasons why.

> **Practice Pointer:**
> If they don't have a favorite book of the Bible it could mean they don't know the Bible that well. Help them learn more.

Preface the Practice:

Ask: "We talked about this a couple of sessions ago, but suppose a guy or girl you really liked wrote you a love letter, would you read it?"

Explain that in the same way, if you really love God, you will be interested in what he has to say to you. The Bible is the most important way he talks to us. The Bible is a miracle book. It cost hundreds of people their lives for us to have it today.

> At this time, hand out the sheets, **God's Amazing Love Letter** (Bible D), to each student. Briefly go over each element of the sheet with the students.

Explain that during this session, the students will divide a chapter of the Bible and study it in its entirety. You want them to understand the importance of studying the Bible **in context**.

Ask: "Have you ever heard of the guy who flipped his Bible open to Matthew 27:5 where it says, "then (Judas) went away and hanged himself", then he flipped to Luke 10:37 where Jesus says, "go and do likewise?"

Explain that reading the scriptures **in context** means we read it like a story - not taking bits and pieces from here and there and trying to put them together to say what we want it to say. It can be a dangerous thing to take scriptures **out of context**.

Modern translations of the Bible read like a book or letter or story - just what it is. It is a good practice to read whole chapters at a time so we can better understand what God is saying to us.

Practice Pointer:
All of the major *cults* use scriptures from the Bible. But they take some out of context and distort the meaning of others. We cannot *pick* and *choose* what we want from the Bible and we cannot ignore what we are not comfortable with in the Bible.

A Promise to Ponder:
All Scripture is God-breathed and is useful for teaching, rebuking, correcting and training in righteousness.   **2 Timothy 3:16**

Practice Makes Perfect:

Explain to the students that, at this time, you are going to divide them into **four** teams. Each team will go into a separate room or area.

They will need to elect a leader for their team and follow the instructions on their **team sheets**, which they will find in their team rooms or areas.

Explain that they will have **15 minutes** in their team time to study their scriptures and prepare their presentations.

Now, divide the students into four teams. Tell them to come back to the main assembly area, ready to make their presentations in 15 minutes.

Practice Pointer:
You can divide your students by numbering them **1** through **4**, or by seating.

A Post-Practice Postlude:

As in every session, compliment the students for their presentations. Don't re-teach what they have just presented, but summarize the chapter you presented.

Encourage them to take home their **God's Amazing Love Letter** hand-out sheets and discuss this session with their parents.

Have your students stand in a circle and join hands. Pray or call on someone to pray. Dismiss.

Bible A

Cut along the dotted line to make a **prompt** instruction sign. Place this sign on the back of a chair near the doorway, with the **prompt** question strips on it. Make sure pens and pencils are available.

Please Take A Slip of Paper and Answer the Question!

Bible B

Make enough copies of this page so each student can
get a **prompt** question slip as they enter the room.
Cut along the dotted lines to make the strips.

Please name your favorite book of the Bible and briefly tell why.

Please name your favorite book of the Bible and briefly tell why.

Please name your favorite book of the Bible and briefly tell why.

Team Sheet C1a   **Philippians 4**   Bible C1

Cut along the dotted line, then give each team its sheet.

Team 1

Pick a leader for your team. He or she will be your spokesperson when you make your presentation. Elect **one team member** to read the scriptures aloud,

         one team member to read the questions,

             and **another team member** to answer them during your presentation.

Make sure all team members are included in some way. You may let **several team members** read or answer.

Your Scripture passage is Philippians 4: 1 - 7. You will have 5 to 7 minutes to make your presentation.

Read verse **1**.
     How does Paul, the writer of this passage, feel about the people at Philippi?

Read verses **2** and **3**.
     What is Paul asking these two women to do? What does he ask the rest of the Christians there to do for them? Why are these requests important?

Read verses **4** and **5**.
     What does "rejoice" mean here? What type of person is he saying we should be in verse **5**?

Read verses **6** and **7**.
     What does "anxious" mean? (It's in the New International Version). Who does he say to take our problems to? What is the "peace of God" he is promising here?

Is there any other comment you wish to make on this passage?

Bible C1

Team Sheet C1b   Philippians 4

Cut along the dotted line, then give each team its sheet.

Team 2

Pick a leader for your team. He or she will be your spokesperson when you make your presentation. Elect **one team member** to read the scriptures aloud,
> **one team member** to read the questions,
> and **one team member** to answer them during your presentation.

Make sure all team members are included in some way. You may let **several team members** read or answer.

Your Scripture passage is Philippians 4: 8 - 9. You will have 5 to 7 minutes to make your presentation.

Read verse **8**.
> Paul, the writer, wants us to think about what is **true, noble, right, pure, lovely, admirable, excellent,** and **praiseworthy.** Why does he want us to think about these things? What kinds of things do you think he is talking about? So, does that mean we *shouldn't* spend time thinking about the *opposite* of these things? Name some things that are the opposite of these things. Why doesn't Paul want us thinking about them?

Read verse **9**.
> Is Paul boasting that he is "all good" when he says to do what you have received or learned from him, or heard or seen him do? (Hint: look up Philippians 3:13, 14). Why would he say such a thing - what did he mean by this?

Is there any other comment you wish to make on this passage?

Bible C1

Team Sheet C1c   Philippians 4

Cut along the dotted line, then give each team its sheet.

Team 3

Pick a leader for your team. He or she will be your spokesperson when you make your presentation. Elect **one team member** to read the scriptures aloud,
> **one team member** to read the questions,
> and **one team member to** answer them during your presentation.

Make sure all team members are included in some way. You may let **several team members** read or answer.

Your Scripture passage is Philippians 4:10 - 13. You will have 5 to 7 minutes to make your presentation.

Read verses **10** and **11**.
> What does Paul, the writer of this passage, mean by, "you have renewed your concern for me." What do you think the Christians at Philippi did that he was rejoicing about? (Hint: read verses 10 through 19 for the answer.)
> See if you can find out where Paul was when he was writing this letter. How could Paul say he was "content" in that circumstance?

Read verse **12**.
> Paul says he knows what it is like to "be in need" and to "have plenty". Does this mean Paul may have been rich or well off at one time? If so, does that mean he gave all that up for the cause of Christ? What do you think Paul thought was more valuable, having a lot of money or having a relationship with Christ?
> What do you think the "secret" was that he found for being content in all situations?

Read verse **13.**
> Is Paul saying he could do *anything* he wanted to - or what God wanted him to do?
> Who is the "him" who gives him strength?
> Do we have access to that same power today or was that just for guys like Paul?

Is there any other comment you wish to make on this passage?

Bible C1

Team Sheet C1d   Philippians 4

Cut along the dotted line, then give each team its sheet.

Team 4

Pick a leader for your team. He or she will be your spokesperson when you make your presentation. Elect **one team member** to read the scriptures aloud,
>**one team member** to read the questions,
>>and **one team member** to answer them during your presentation.

Make sure all team members are involved in some way. You may let **several team members** read or answer.

Your Scripture passage is Philippians 4: 14 - 23. You will have 5 to 7 minutes to make your presentation.

Read verses **14** through **18**.
>What is Paul, the writer of the passage, talking about in these verses? (Hint: you might need to read verses 10 through 19 to get the whole picture.) Is there a lesson we can learn from the Christians at Philippi about how they continually gave gifts to Paul - a missionary? He said their offering was "pleasing to God". Who is Paul saying a gift to a minister or church or missionary is really a gift for?

Read verse **19**.
>He was just talking about them giving *him* gifts, why is he now saying God would supply *their* needs? What is this verse promising Christians today? What is the difference between our *wants* and our *needs*? Does God care about the things we *want*?

Read verses **20** through **23**.
>Who does Paul want all glory to go to, according to verse **20**? Why do we have these "good-bys" in the Bible?

Is there any other comment you wish to make on this passage?

Bible C2

Team Sheet C2a   Ephesians 6

Cut along the dotted line, then give each team its sheet.

Team 1

Pick a leader for your team. He or she will be your spokesperson when you make your presentation. Elect **one team member** to read the scriptures aloud,
> **one team member** to read the questions,
> and **another team member** to answer them during your presentation.

Make sure all team members are included in some way. You may let **several team members** read and answer.

Your Scripture passage is Ephesians 6: 1 - 4. You will have 5 to 7 minutes to make your presentation.

Read verse **1**.
> Why does he say children should obey their parents?

Read verses **2** and **3**.
> What is Paul, the writer of this book, quoting when he says, "Honor your father and mother"? What is the promise attached to that commandment? What does God mean by that promise?

Read verse **4**.
> What does "exasperate" (NIV) mean? Why would he say such a thing to fathers? Fathers, bring up your children "in the training and instruction of the Lord" - what does that mean?

Is there any other comment you with to make on this passage?

Bible C2

Team Sheet C2b   Ephesians 6

Cut along the dotted line, then give each team its sheet.

Team 2

Pick a leader for your team. He or she will be your spokesperson when you make your presentation. Elect **one team member** to read the scriptures aloud,
>   **one team member** to read the questions,
>> and **one team member** to answer them during your presentation.

Make sure all team members are included in some way. You may let **several team members** read or answer.

Your Scripture passage is Ephesians 6: 5 - 9. You will have 5 to 7 minutes to make your presentation.

Read verse **5**.
> Why would Paul, the writer of this book, be talking about slaves? Is he saying slavery is right? Why should slaves obey their masters? Is there any modern application you can make from this verse?

Read verses **6** and **7**.
> When we serve some person, who does Paul say we are really serving?

Read verse **8**.
> Is Paul saying that God judges everyone the same or differently in this verse? Does it matter to God whether you are rich or poor, slave or free?

Read verse **9**.
> How does Paul say for masters to treat their slaves? Is there any modern application you can make from this verse?

Is there any other comment you wish to make on this passage?

Bible C2

Team Sheet C2c   Ephesians 6

Cut along the dotted line, then give each team its sheet.

Team 3

Pick a leader for your team. He or she will be your spokesperson when you make your presentation. Elect **one team member** to read the scriptures aloud,
> **one team member** to read the questions,
> and **one team member** to answer them during the presentation.

Make sure all team members are included in some way. You may let **several team members** read or answer. You may want to let **different team members** tell what each piece of armor is.

Your Scripture passage is Ephesians 6:10 - 17. You will have 5 to 7 minutes to make your presentation.

Read verse **10**.
> Does Paul, the writer of this passage, say we should be *weak* or *strong*? Where does that strength come from?

Read verses **11** and **12** and **13**.
> Who do we fight against? Is Paul saying we are in *spiritual warfare*?
> What does Paul say to put on so we can "take our stand"?

Read verses **14** through **17**.
> What is the **belt**?
> What is the **breastplate**?
> What are the **shoes**?
> What is the **shield**?
> What is the **helmet**?
> What is the **sword**?

Is there any other comment you wish to make on this passage?

Bible C2

Team Sheet C2d   Ephesians 6

Cut along the dotted line, then give each team its sheet.

Team 4

Pick a leader for your team. He or she will be your spokesperson when you make your presentation. Elect **one team member** to read the scriptures aloud,
> **one team member** to read the questions,
> > and **one team member** to answer them during your presentation.

Make sure all team members are included in some way. You may let **several team members** read or answer.

Your Scripture passage is Ephesians 6: 18 - 23. You will have 5 to 7 minutes to make your presentation.

Read verse **18**.
> Paul, the writer of this passage, says to do something *three different times* in this one verse - what is it? How important did Paul think prayer was? Do you think prayer is still that important today?

Read verse **19** and **20**.
> Who is Paul asking them to pray for in these verses? What is it Paul is asking them to pray for him for in verse **20**? What does he mean by, "ambassador in chains"?

Read verses **21** through **23**.
> Why does Paul say he is sending Tychicus to them?

Is there any other comment you wish to make on this passage?

Bible D

Make enough copies of the following page for each student.

God's Amazing Love Letter - The Bible!

The Bible is the most incredible, miraculous, wonderful book ever written. It is actually a whole library of 66 books. (The Christian-Protestant Canon). It's God's love letter to us!

It was:

>Written over a period of nearly 1500 years.
>Written on three different continents.
>Written by as many as 40 authors - including fishermen, a cup bearer to the king, shepherds, farmers, rabbis, a tax collector, a doctor, poets, kings, preachers and prisoners.
>Written in three different languages: Hebrew, Greek and Aramaic.

It contains stories about:

>War and peace, romance, suspense, family struggles, mystery, murder, rape, revenge, escapes, danger, heartache, paradise, prisoners, slaves, kings, princes, prophets, births, deaths, money, poverty, spies, traitors, bullies, friends, enemies, heroes, adultery, forgiveness, faith, hope, love, hate, sinners and a savior.

It contains:

>Poetry, prose, prophecy, history, sermons, love stories, laws, personal and public letters. It contains every element of the human condition. But yet, it is also a *single* story about Paradise - lost in Genesis, then regained in Revelation. There is a message of hope throughout every book: the blood sacrifice and redemption of Jesus, who made us friends again with the Father by paying the price for our sins - something we could not do ourselves.

The Chapters and Verses were divided and numbered by the Archbishop of Canterbury, Stephen Langton, in 1228. It was first translated into English in 1382 and was the first book ever to be mass-published by a printing press in 1455. It is the number one selling and read book of all times. It is full of thousands of controversial issues and all of the authors agree upon them - a miracle in itself. More manuscripts have been found proving its authenticity than any other book from antiquity. The Bible - you can read it, believe it and stake your life on it.

7

Session Seven: Self-Esteem Practice

_____

_____

A Peek at the Practice:
By the end of this session, you will have taught your students the importance of building-up and encouraging one another and how damaging it can be to put each other down. The youth will have then practiced encouraging, forgiving and apologizing to one other.

The Primary Objective Points:

Students Will:

- Learn the importance of building-up and encouraging one another.

- Consider the importance of forgiving one another from a Biblical perspective.

- Actually practice encouraging and apologizing to their peers.

Plan Ahead:

Read through the lesson plan. Personalize it to fit your group's personality. Make any adjustments you deem necessary to fit the size and makeup of your group.

Make copies of the **prompt** question sheets (Self B), then cut them into strips along the dotted lines. Make enough strips for each student. Have pens or pencils available for each student's use.

Make enough copies of **Four Twenty-Nine** (Self C) for each student.

Place the students' chairs in a circle.

Pray for your students and for the teaching of this session. Ask yourself: do *I* make sure the things I say to my students, friends and family members build them up? Start today being more careful with what you say.

Set a chair by the doorway so students will pass by it as they enter. Place the **prompt** questions strips on it. Tape the sign, "Please take a sheet and answer the question" (Self A) on the back of the chair. Make sure pens or pencils are there as well.

*Note: You may need to hand out **Teaching Topics** for *Session Eight* at the end of this session.

Prompt Your Young People:

As the students enter the room, they will take a **prompt** question strip and answer the question. Take up the strips or have a volunteer do so.

Begin your session as you are most comfortable: Make needed announcements, sing songs, etc.

> **Practice Pointer:**
> This is a good session to sing songs about friendship and "leaning on each other..." Any song about being friends or brothers and sisters would work well with this session.

Sort through the **prompt** questions strips and read a variety of answers. Always remember to never criticize or put down your students' answers.

Allow for comments on the answers.

Brag on your students' answers. Agree with them on their positive points about themselves. The more you brag on your students, the better - but remember, they can see right through you if you are not sincere!

> **Practice Pointer:**
> It may be hard for some youth to say something good about themselves. You may have to help them out a little.

Preface the Practice:

Ask: "You may have heard the old saying, 'sticks and stones can break my bones, but words will never hurt me'. Do you believe this saying is true?"

Let them discuss this statement and how true it is. Explain to them that words can hurt just as deeply as any stick - words can even kill. Some young people have been put down so often they actually believe they are worthless. Some have committed suicide, others have never risen to their fullest potential because of hurtful words.

Ask: "What if you are just kidding around and the person knows you are, can that still hurt him?"

Explain that anytime we have fun at someone else's expense, no matter how harmless it seems, we can hurt him deeply. An overweight person may be a good sport about the jokes and funny names, but it adds up to hurting his feelings and self-esteem.

Ask: "Why do you think young people always put each other down and pick on the faults of others?"

Explain that young people are finding their own identities and many are unsure of themselves. When we put others down it is usually so that *we* will look good in others' eyes - and also in our own.

Have someone read Galatians 5:15.

This scripture says "If you keep on biting and devouring each other, watch out or you will be destroyed by each other."

If you put a bunch of little chickens in a coop and one of them gets injured - perhaps nicked on a snag in the chicken wire - the rest of them will pick at the wound until they kill the chick. This is what Paul is talking about. A Christian who has a flaw (and don't we all) needs love, nurturing and acceptance for who he is. What he doesn't need is to be constantly reminded and "picked on" about his flaw. A Christian who has committed some sin (and don't we all) needs to be gently brought back, loved and accepted for who he *still* is in Christ. What he doesn't need is to be "kicked when he is down." Yet, that is exactly what we often do.

Practice Pointer:
Gossip is a way of life for many teenagers - and adults. It is hard to stop and it is hard not to listen too, but it is always at someone's expense - and always hurts someone. Often, Christians will say, "we need to pray for so and so, she's living in sin." That's not a prayer request, that's gossip!

Have someone go back one scripture and read Galatians 5:14.

To "love our neighbor as ourselves" means to treat others as you would want them to treat you. God wants us to love ourselves - how can you love someone else if you don't love yourself? What does that mean? It means you understand that you are created and loved by God and you have value. God doesn't make junk and he doesn't make mistakes. When you feel good about who you are you can start giving of yourself to help others feel good about themselves, too. The Bible always teaches to put others first and not to "think more highly of yourself than you should." This doesn't mean we should put ourselves down, it simply means we should always think of the other person's needs and feelings. Jesus put the needs of the whole world above his own, then forgave us for what we did to him.

Practice Pointer:
Romans 12:3. Paul goes on to say in this passage that we are all one body and that we are all in this together - and we need to help one another.

Have someone read Ephesians 4:29.

Explain that "unwholesome" talk is anything that is impure, unholy or would bring someone else down. We should *not* say things that will hurt others, but we *should* say things that will help them. Saying nice things about others is a real problem for lots of teenagers because they don't feel good enough about themselves to say something good about someone else. When we catch on to how much God loves us, just like we are, then we can start giving that love to others. You cannot give what you do not have.

Practice Pointer:
In our youth group, we say, **"four twenty-nine"** when someone starts putting someone else down (see Self C).

Ask: "So, what if others put *you* down about something - should you forgive them?"

Explain that this is the other side of the coin. We shouldn't put others down - but if others put *us* down, we need to forgive them - just like Jesus forgives us.

In **Matthew 18:21 - 35**, Jesus tells us to keep on forgiving others when they wrong us. He tells the parable of the servant who was forgiven of a debt of a million dollars but wouldn't forgive a fellow servant who owed him about twenty dollars! The king threw him in prison to be tortured for the rest of his life. *We* are the ones who suffer when we don't forgive. It hurts our relationship with God and that hatred keeps us "in prison". Jesus said in **Matthew 6:14 - 15**, that we must forgive others if God is going to forgive us. God makes it very clear that Christians must forgive others.

Practice Pointer:
Often, our first reaction is to get *revenge* when someone hurts us. The Bible teaches over and over that revenge is not the Christian response. See **Matthew 5:38 - 42** and **Romans 12:17 - 21**.

Ask: "So, if you have hurt someone with the things you have said about him, should you apologize or just let it go?"

Explain that our relationship with others directly affects our relationship with God. Jesus said in **Matthew 5: 23 - 24**, that we should not make an offering to God if we know another Christian is upset with us. He said to first be *reconciled* - remember that word? It means to be made friends again. When you hurt someone, the Christian thing to do is to apologize to him and restore your friendship.

Note: get into a circle at this time if you have not already done so.

Practice Pointer:
I don't think it's helpful or appropriate for young people to apologize for *feelings* they hold against someone - especially if that person doesn't even know it. Apologies should be made to those we said or did something to. If it was said in public, a public apology may be called for; if it was said in private, then a private apology is probably more appropriate. The apology should never cause more pain than the original act or feeling.

A Promise to Ponder:
A tongue that brings healing is a tree of life, but a deceitful tongue crushes the spirit.
Proverbs 15:4

Practice Makes Perfect:

Explain to the students that giving compliments doesn't come naturally to most people - it takes practice. For some, it is very difficult to say good things about others - but that's exactly what Christ would have us do.

You, the leader, will go first. Turn to the person on your right and say one thing you really like about that person. It must be a genuine, sincere compliment:

> **"You have always been there when I needed to talk to someone."**
>
> **"I don't really know you that well, but you seem like a really nice, honest person."**
>
> **"I think you have a really friendly personality and I know you make good grades at school."**
>
> **"You are always here at church and I have always looked up to you because you act like I think a Christian should."**

Some examples of what is *not* a real compliment:

> **"Cool shirt."**
>
> **"Nice shoes."**

Also, watch out for "veiled put-downs". These sound at first like a compliment, but are actually putting the person down:

> **"You're a fairly nice looking girl, even if you are too tall."**

Practice Pointer:
You might be thinking at this point, "I can just see my junior high guys giving a real compliment to each other." But they want someone to say something nice about *them* so they will do their part. They may want to joke around at first, but they will come around when they realize they are about to be complimented.

After you have complimented the person on your right, that person will compliment the person on his right and so on around the circle. If you finish and have plenty of time left, you may want to go *left* around the circle.

After the youth have all given and received a compliment, open the floor for them to compliment anyone they choose. Just make sure the same person isn't being praised over and over.

Now that they are "loosened up" a bit, ask if anyone needs to **apologize** to someone or to tell someone that they **forgive** them. **Remember, private matters need to be handled that way - in private.** But if someone needs to make a public apology, this would be a good time. If they have a *private* apology, they can ask the person to go into a classroom or out into the hall.

Practice Pointer:
If you choose to include this part of the practice into your session, please be careful. Again, more harm can be done than the students know if they start telling someone that they "just don't like them". You will need to keep the students focused on genuine apologies and forgiveness. This is not a time to air hurtful feelings that they plan to do nothing about.

Practice Pointer:
From a practical standpoint, forgiveness means you no longer hold a grudge against someone who hurt you. You will speak to him again and interact with him again. You no longer wish to take some form of revenge on him. Forgiveness means you eventually forget that he ever hurt you and feel for him as though he never did. This is the way God forgives us. God *doesn't* say, "I'll forgive him, but I won't forget what he did to me!" That is not real forgiveness.

A Post-Practice Postlude:

You will be the judge as to how and when this session should end. They may begin to weep and get really honest with each other. That's okay. But you will know when it becomes time to close it down. As always, brag on your students for their participation and for their honesty.

Hand out the sheet, **Four Twenty-Nine** (Self C), and encourage them to memorize the scriptures on it and discuss them and this session with their parents.

Have your students stand in a circle and join hands. Pray or call on someone to pray. Dismiss.

Self A

Cut along the dotted line to make a **prompt** instruction sign. Place this sign on the back of a chair near the doorway, with the **prompt** question strips on it. Make sure pens and pencils are available.

PLEASE TAKE A SLIP OF PAPER AND ANSWER THE QUESTION!

Self B

Make enough copies of this page so that each student
can get a **prompt** question strip as they enter the room.
Cut along the dotted lines to make the strips.

Name one thing that you really like about yourself.

Name one thing that you really like about yourself.

Name one thing that you really like about yourself.

Self C

Cut along the dotted line then make enough copies of this sheet for each student.

Four Twenty-Nine!

"Do not let any unwholesome talk come out of your mouths, but only what is helpful for building others up according to their needs, that it may benefit those who listen."

Ephesians 4:29

Memorize this scripture and then anytime you start to say something that isn't nice about someone, say to yourself, "four twenty-nine". Then don't say what it was you were about to say that you know you shouldn't say. You know?

"If you keep on biting and devouring each other, watch out or you will be destroyed by each other."

Galatians 5:15

If you put a bunch of little chickens in a pen together and one of them gets injured - you know, on a nail or something - the rest of them will "pick on" the wound until they actually kill the poor chick. Whoa! Don't kick your friends when they are down, but work on helping and encouraging them.

8

Session Eight: Teaching Practice

A Peek at the Practice:
By the end of this session, you will have shown your students the importance of discipling others and will have led three of them to actually practice teaching.

The Primary Objective Points:

Students Will:

- Learn the importance of discipling and teaching other students.

- Study Biblical truths about who should teach and who should disciple.

- Three students of your choosing will teach the rest of the group.

121

Plan Ahead:

Read through the lesson plan. Personalize it to fit your group's personality. Make any adjustments you deem necessary to fit the size and makeup of your group.

You will need to advise your "teachers" - the students who will be teaching during this session - in advance. You may need to tell them a week in advance or, at least, several days.

Make copies of the **prompt** question sheets (Teaching B), then cut them into strips along the dotted lines. Make enough strips for each student. Have pens or pencils ready for each student's use.

Choose and make copies of the **Teaching Topics** teaching sheets (Teaching C1 - C2). You will give one Teaching Instruction Sheet (Teaching C1a - C2c) to each student who will be teaching. If you choose to let a *team* teach each sheet, give each team member a teaching sheet.
(This session is designed for only one or two teachers per team sheet.)

Select three "teachers" from among the students, in advance, and give them their Teaching Instruction Sheets **in advance**. Again, make sure the students you choose will be there for the session and can handle the task.

Pray for your students, especially those who will be teaching, and for this session. You want to equip and enable your students to disciple others, while being careful not interfere or discourage.

> **Practice Pointer:**
> You will need to be selective about who you choose to teach during this session. Make sure the students will *be there* on the day of the session - and make sure they are able to handle the task. On the other hand, try giving students who are not always leading out a chance - they may be the ones who will surprise you and who may need this the most. Pray for God's guidance on this matter.

> **Practice Pointer:**
> If you give your students their teaching sheets too far in advance, their chances will be greater of not being there for the session. A week or even a half of a week should be about right.

Set a chair by the doorway so students will pass by it as they enter. Place the **prompt** question strips on it. Tape the sign "Please take a slip of paper and answer the question" (Teaching A) on the back of the chair.

Prompt Your Young People:

As the students enter the room, they will take a **prompt** question strip and answer the question. Take up the strips or have a volunteer do so.

Begin your session time as you are most comfortable: Make needed announcements, sing songs, etc.

Next, take prayer requests. Pray, or call on someone to pray.

Sort through the **prompt** question strips and read a variety of answers to the students. This should be fairly light-hearted, but be careful that you don't allow *making fun of* their former teachers.

Get students to elaborate on why they liked a certain teacher.

Be careful not to spend too much time on this part of the session, you want to give your "teachers" time to teach.

Practice Pointer:
What you are looking for here is *why* they liked certain teachers - their enthusiasm, style, sense of humor, how well they taught, etc.

Preface the Practice:

Ask: "Do you think it is important for young people to be able to teach in front of other young people?"

Explain that it is important for a couple of reasons:

    First: It is good for a student to speak and teach in front of his peers for *that student's* sake. The teacher always learns more than his students and the preparation is excellent Bible study. A student will retain most of what he teaches - simply because he studied and prepared for it, then taught it aloud.

    Second: It is good for the other students. Students like to hear from their peers. Often, students will listen to their peers when they may tune out adults. This is because student teachers are where they are now, know what they are going through, and talk in their own language. Student teachers can be very direct about relevant issues and the group will almost always listen to - *and remember* - what they say.

Practice Pointer:
Don't spend too much time on this part of the session - the idea is to run through this quickly, then give enough time to your "teachers" to teach. Spend only 5 to 10 minutes here, depending on how much time you have. The three teachers will need 10 minutes each for a total of **30 minutes**.

Ask: "If a person is going to teach when he is an adult, when do you think he should start?"

Obviously, the sooner a person starts practicing *anything*, the better that person can become at it. Teaching is no different. Also, students may find they really like to teach, once they try it. God uses sessions just like this one to show young people he has gifted them to teach. Paul told Timothy not to let people "look down on him" because he was young - today's youth need to be discipling others - and setting an example for them - as soon as they become Christians.

Practice Pointer:
1 Timothy 4:12

Ask: "So, do you think every Christian should teach others?"

The Bible says no. James said, *"Not many of you should presume to be teachers, my brothers, because you know that we who teach will be judged more strictly."* **James 3:1**

When a student or adult stands to teach, they must back up what they say with their lives. Teaching is an honor and privilege reserved for those who are willing to practice what they preach. A teacher can do more harm than good if he says one thing but does another. People are more interested in what we *do* than what we *say*. James goes on to say that no one is perfect, but those who teach will be judged more strictly - and rightly so.

All Christians should *disciple* others, however. Jesus said in **Matthew 28:19 -20**, "Go and make disciples of all nations..."

A disciple is a learner - a student. The difference is that Christians should help each other be more like Christ. We just shouldn't stand in front of a group and teach unless we can back-up what we say with the way we try to live our lives.

Help your students to see that they *are* teaching others, whether they realize it or not: Younger students and weaker Christians are watching them and they should be very careful how they act because of that.

> **Practice Pointer:**
> You will want to note this verse as you select your student teachers for this session. The students don't have to be the brightest and most outgoing - but they *do* need to be students who are at least trying to live their lives for God. No student is perfect, but as James says, teachers will be judged more strictly.

> ## A Promise To Ponder:
> "All authority in heaven and on earth has been given to me. Therefore go and make disciples of all nations, baptizing them in the name of the Father and of the Son and of the Holy Spirit, and teaching them to obey everything I have commanded you. And surely I am with you always, even to the very end of the age."

Practice Makes Perfect:

At this time, your "teachers" will come to the front of the group and teach the rest of the students.

You will want to gauge your time, to help keep the students within their time allotment.

You may want to pray again - for the student teachers.

A Post-Practice Postlude:

If time permits, wrap-up the lessons with a concluding sentence or two - don't *reteach* what your students have just taught.

Brag on your "teachers". Try to mention a strong point or two from each one, but be sincere.

Never criticize or put-down any student in any form, either veiled or blatant.

Your students probably missed some points you would have liked for them to cover - and they might have said some things you wouldn't have thought of. That's okay. Again, don't try to reteach the lessons - since that is a form of putting them down.

Pray. Dismiss.

Teaching A

Cut along the dotted line to make a **Prompt** instruction sign. Place this sign on the back of a chair near the doorway, with the **prompt** questions strips on it. Make sure pens or pencils are available.

Please Take A Slip of Paper and Answer the Question!

Teaching B

Make enough copies of this page so that each student can get a **prompt** question strip as they enter the room. Cut along the dotted lines to make the strips.

Name your favorite School Teacher you've ever had. Why did you like this teacher?

Name your favorite School Teacher you've ever had. Why did you like this teacher?

Name your favorite School Teacher you've ever had. Why did you like this teacher?

Teaching C1a

Teaching Topic - 1: Worship

Choose a teaching topic. (C1 or C2)
Make a copy of this teaching sheet. Cut along the dotted lines. Give the sheet to the appropriate "teacher" in advance of the session.

Teaching Instruction Sheet

Topic: <u>Our Response to God: Worship.</u>
Teacher Number **1**
Time allotment: 10 minutes
Text: Job 1:1 - 21

Advance Preparation:
Read Job 1:1 - 21. Consider the following elements of this passage:
What was Job (pronounced *Jobe*) like? What did God ask Satan? What was Satan's accusation against Job? What did God allow Satan to do to Job? What was Job's response in verses 20 and 21?

Teaching the Session:
1. Tell the story in this passage in your own words.
2. Read, then **answer** the following questions in front of the group:
   a. Did Job deserve what happened to him? Why or why not?
   _____
   b. Why do you think God allowed such terrible things to happen to Job? _____
   c. What was Job's response to all the bad news? _____
   _____ What might some people's have been?
   _____
   d. Does God still allow bad things to happen to good people today? _____ According to this passage, what should our response be? _____
   e. Do you think very many people can respond to God like Job did?
   _____

Teaching C1b
Teaching Topic - 1: Worship

Make a copy of this teaching sheet. Cut along the dotted lines. Give the sheet to the appropriate "teacher" in advance of the session.

Teaching Instruction Sheet

Topic: <u>Our Response to God: Worship</u>
Teacher Number **2**
Time allotment: 10 minutes
Text: 2 Samuel 11:1 - 27, 12:13 - 20

Advance Preparation:
Read 2 Samuel 11:1 - 27, 12:13 - 20. Consider the following elements of this passage: What sins did David commit in this passage? Could Bathsheba have stopped what happened to her? Did Uriah deserve what happened to him? Did David and Bathsheba's baby deserve what happened to him? What was David's attitude toward God when the child died?

Teaching the Session:
1. Tell the story in this passage in your own words.
2. Read, then **answer** the following questions in front of the group:

   a. How many of the "Ten Commandments" did David break in this story?
   _____

   b. Was David sorry for his actions? _____ How did God punish David for his sins? _____

   c. How many people suffered because of David's sins? Name them. _____
   _____

   d. Do you think it was fair to punish David so harshly? _____

   e. What was David's response to God after the child died? _____
   _____

   f. Based on this passage, what should our response be when bad things happen?
   _____

Teaching C1c

Teaching Topic - 1: Worship

Make a copy of this teaching sheet. Cut along the dotted line. Give the sheet to the appropriate "teacher" in advance of the session.

Teaching Instruction Sheet

Topic: <u>Our Response to God: Worship</u>
Teacher Number **3**
Time allotment: 10 minutes
Text: Luke 17: 11 - 17

Advance Preparation:
Read Luke 17: 11 - 17. Consider the following elements of this passage:
How many men did Jesus heal in this passage? How many came back to thank him? What is *leprosy*? What does it do to you? Is it fatal? When were the men healed, according to the passage?

Teaching the Session:
1. Tell the story in this passage in your own words.
2. Read, then **answer** the following questions in front of the group:
    a. How many men did Jesus heal of their leprosy that day? _____
    b. How many men returned to thank him? _____
    c. Why do you think the other nine *didn't* come back to thank Jesus?
    _____
    d. Do you think a lot of people take Jesus' goodness for granted today? _____
    e. According to this passage, what is the proper response when we realize Jesus has blessed us? _____

Teaching C2a

Teaching Topic - 2: Jonah

Choose a teaching topic (C1 or C2). Make a copy of this teaching sheet. Cut along the dotted line. Give the sheet to the appropriate "teacher" in advance of the session.

Teaching Instruction Sheet

Topic: <u>Jonah</u>
Teacher Number **1**
Time allotment: 10 minutes
Text: Jonah 1:1 - 17

Advance Preparation:
Read the first chapter of Jonah. Consider the following elements of this passage:
> What did God tell Jonah to do? What did Jonah do when told? What happened while he was on the boat? What did he tell the sailors to do to him? Why? What happened to Jonah next? How did the men on the boat respond to the calmness?

Teaching the Session:
1. Tell the story in the passage in your own words.
2. Read, then **answer** the following questions in front of the group:
    a. What did God tell Jonah to do? _____
    b. What did Jonah do instead? _____
    c. What happened while he was in the boat? _____
    d. What did he tell the sailors to do to him? _____
    e. What happened to Jonah next? _____
    f. How did the sailors respond, when they saw God at work? _____
    g. What does Jonah have in common with Jesus, according to this passage?
    _____

(Hint: 3 days and 3 nights, and a stormy boat ride!)

Teaching C2b

Teaching Topic - 2: Jonah

Make a copy of this teaching sheet. Cut along the dotted line. Give the sheet to the appropriate "teacher" in advance of the session.

Teaching Instruction Sheet

Topic: <u>Jonah</u>
Teacher Number **2**
Time allotment: 10 minutes
Text: Jonah 2:10, 3: 1 - 10

Advance Preparation:
Read the Jonah 2:10, 3:1 - 10. You will need to read the first chapter to fully understand this one. Consider the following elements of this passage:
    What did the fish do with Jonah? What did God tell Jonah to do? What did Jonah do this time? What was Jonah's message to Nineveh? What was their response? What was God's response to their repentance?

Teaching the Session:
1. Tell the story of this passage in your own words.
2. Read, then **answer** the following questions in front of the group:
    a. What did the fish do with Jonah? _____
    b. What did God ask Jonah to do?_____
    c. What was Jonah's response this time? _____
    d. Why do you think Jonah obeyed this time? _____
_____
    e. What was Jonah's message to the people of Nineveh? _____
    f. What was their response? _____
    g. What was God's response to their repentance? _____
    h. What does this say about God's mercy to "sinners"? _____
    I. What would have happened to the people of Nineveh if Jonah had continued to be disobedient? _____

Teaching C2c

Teaching Topic - 2 : Jonah

Make a copy of this teaching sheet. Cut along the dotted line. Give the sheet to the appropriate "teacher" in advance of the session.

Teaching Instruction Sheet

Topic: Jonah
Teacher Number **3**
Time allotment: 10 minutes
Text: Jonah 4: 1 - 11

Advance Preparation:
Read the fourth chapter of Jonah. You will need to read the whole book to understand this chapter. Consider the following elements of this passage:
What was Jonah's reaction to the people of Nineveh's repentance? What did he do next? What did God do to ease his suffering? Then what happened to the vine? What was Jonah's reaction to this? What was God teaching Jonah with the vine and the worm, according to the passage?

Teaching the Session:
1. Tell the story of this chapter in your own words.
2. Read, then **answer** the following questions in front of the group:
    a. What was Jonah's response to God's mercy on the people of Nineveh?_____ _____ Why do you think he reacted that way? _____

    b. Do you think Jonah had a right to be mad that 120-thousand people were spared? _____ Why was Jonah more concerned about one vine than all of those people? _____

    c. Do Christians today sometimes get mad when God has mercy on our "enemies"? _____
    d. What does this story tell about the mercy of God? _____

9

Session Nine: Obedience Practice

___

A Peek at the Practice:
By the end of this session, you will have taught your students the importance of unquestioned obedience to God and will have led them to practice their faith and obedience.

The Primary Objective Points:

Students Will:

- Learn the importance of obedience to God.

- Study examples of Biblical characters who demonstrated their faith by their obedience to God.

- Actually practice being obedient to God by acting-out obedience in a role-play situation.

Plan Ahead:

Read through the lesson plan. Personalize it to fit your group's personality. Make any adjustments you deem necessary to fit the size and makeup of your group.

You may need a small amount of preparation in advance for some of the **Obedience Team Ideas (C1 - C6)** to work properly. You will divide your students into teams and each team will perform some act of obedience that may seem silly to them at the time. *This is the whole point of this session!* Look over the **Obedience Team Ideas** (Obey C1 - C6) and choose **three** of them. See what supplies you would need for the ones you choose.

Make copies of the **prompt** question sheets (Obey B), then cut them into strips along the dotted lines. Make enough strips for each student. Have pens or pencils available for each student's use.

Make enough copies of the **Obedience Rules!** handout sheet (Obey D) for each student.

Copy the **Obedience Team** door signs (Obey E) onto colorful paper and place them on the room doors (or areas) to designate where each team will meet.

Make a copy of the **Obedience Team Ideas** (Obey C1 - C6) you have selected for each team leader.

Pray for your students and for this session. *What is your attitude about complete obedience to God?*

Set a chair by the doorway so students will pass by it as they enter. Place the **prompt** question strips on it. Tape the sign "Please take a slip of paper and answer the Question" (Obey A) on the back of the chair.

Prompt Your Young People:

As the students enter the room, they will take a **prompt** question strip and answer the question. Take up the strips or have a volunteer do so.

Begin your session time as you are most comfortable: Make needed announcements, sing songs, etc.

Next, take prayer requests. Pray, or call on someone to pray.

Sort through the **prompt** question strips and read a variety of answers to the students. Again, never criticize the students' answers.

Allow for comments on the answers.

Brag on your students for their answers - but always with sincerity.

Preface the Practice:

Ask: "Why do you think it is important to God that we are obedient to Him?"

Explain that Jesus said we would obey Him if we loved him (**John 14:14**) - and obviously, we must love Him. God demands that we trust Him and do what He asks us in his Word (the Bible). The Bible says it is impossible to please God without faith in Him (**Hebrews 11:6**). Our relationship with God must be based on doing what He tells us - whether or not it makes sense to us.

Practice Pointer:
Carefully gage your time during this session. You will need **45 minutes** once the practice begins to complete the task at hand.

Ask: "But what if God asks us to do something that seems really silly or dumb?"

He told Noah to build a big boat in the desert. He told Abraham to pack up and leave home. He told Joshua to march around Jericho for a week blowing trumpets. *He tells us to turn the other cheek when struck.*

We must come to the place where we admit that God is smarter than us and knows what's best for us. Until we do, we will never please God and will never be blessed like He wants to bless us.

Ask: "Was Jesus obedient to God?"

Practice Pointer:
God generally tells us what to do through the Bible in this, the New Testament Church age. Students shouldn't be concerned about hearing specific commands from Him - except for when the Holy Spirit prompts them to witness or obey God in some other way that is already commanded in the Bible. In the same way, God would never tell us to do anything that would be contrary to what the Bible says.

Clearly He was. He prayed, "Your will be done on Earth as it is in Heaven" (**Matthew 6:10**), which as we discuss in the first session, is about being obedient. He prayed, "not as I will, but as you will" (**Matthew 26:39**) just before he was arrested and crucified for our sins. Paul says Jesus was "obedient to death - even death on a cross" (**Philippians 1:8**). Jesus is always our one and only example.

In the "Faith Hall of Fame" found in **Hebrews 11**, the writer explains the connection between faith, obedience and being used and blessed by God.

We simply must obey God if we believe in Him.

A Promise to Ponder:
"...but showing love to a thousand generations of those who love me and keep my commandments." **Exodus 20:6**

Practice Makes Perfect:

Explain that at this time you are going to divide your students into **three** teams. Each team will go to an assigned room (or area) and follow the instructions that will be given to them (the **Obedience Team Ideas** sheet).
>Either **you** choose a team leader for each team or tell the **teams** to choose when they meet together.

Tell them to read and follow their instructions to the letter.

> They will stay in the room with their teams for **15 minutes.** They will then come back to the main assembly area to perform their assigned tasks.

You can divide the students by **numbering** them or by section, depending on if you want them to be on teams with the friends they are sitting by.

Now, divide them into teams and give the Obedience Team Ideas Sheet to the team leaders. They will need to all meet back together in the main assembly area in 15 minutes.

Each team will need about 10 minutes once they return - so make sure you have 30 to 40 minutes for their presentations and your wrap-up. You need, then, 45 minutes from this point.

A Post-Practice Postlude:

As in every session, compliment the students for their presentations. Tell them how proud you are of their obedience - in following the instructions. Remind them that we need to be obedient to God and to God's Word, no matter whether or not it makes sense to us. God is *so* much smarter than us - and He is always interested in what's best for us!

Hand out the **Obedience Rules!** sheets (Obey D) to the students and encourage them to read it and discuss it and this session with their parents.

Pray or call on someone to pray. Dismiss.

Obey A

Cut along the dotted line to make a **prompt** instruction sign. Place this sign on the back of a chair near the doorway, with the **prompt** questions strips on it. Make sure pens or pencils are available.

Please Take A Slip of Paper and Answer the Question!

Obey B

Make enough copies of this page so that each student
can get a **prompt** question strip as they enter the room.
Cut along the dotted lines to make the strips.

Briefly tell us about a time when you disobeyed your parents and got caught - and what happened to you because of it.

Briefly tell us about a time when you disobeyed your parents and got caught - and what happened to you because of it.

Briefly tell us about a time when you disobeyed your parents and got caught - and what happened to you because of it.

Obey C1
Obedience Team Ideas

Choose three **Obedience Team Ideas**. Make a copy for the team leader.
Cut along the dotted line and give the sheets to the leaders.

Abraham Leaves Home

Read Genesis 12:1 - 5.   <u>Carefully follow these instructions</u>:

1. Answer among yourselves the following questions:
   How would you feel if God told you to pack your stuff and leave your friends and family?
   What was Abram's (Abraham's) response in verse 4?
   How did God bless Abraham because Abraham obeyed God?

2. Now, gather all of your stuff (Bibles, purses, notebooks, jackets...) and one folding chair. Quietly carry your stuff one lap around the church. (If it's raining, up to the far end of the church and back twice.) Don't talk to anyone while you walk, but think about how God wants you to go into some uncomfortable places sometimes for Him: like visiting sick friends, nursing homes, mission trips, witnessing, etc. Are you obedient like Abraham was?

3. When you get back to the room, go to the main assembly area and wait for the other students to assemble. Then have a spokesperson go to the front (when it's your turn) and tell about what you just did. Have him or her tell about the passage you read and what Abraham did. (Abraham became the "Father of the Jewish Nation" and his offspring - Jesus - has blessed the whole world - all because he was obedient!)

Obey C2
Obedience Team Ideas

Jesus, Obedient even to Death

Read Philippians 2:5 - 11. <u>Carefully follow these instructions:</u>
1. Answer among yourselves the following questions:
   How hard do you think it was for Jesus to leave comfortable Heaven to come to hot, smelly, dirty Earth, born in a barn?
   How hard was for Him to live as a homeless man, never marry, be persecuted, then die a brutal, bloody death on a cross for something He didn't do?
   Does the passage say Jesus was obedient to God? Where?
   How obedient? If Jesus was obedient, should we be? Why?
   How does the passage say God has honored Jesus because of His Obedience?

2. Find the words to the first verse of the old hymn, "The Old Rugged Cross" if you have to go find a hymnal in the sanctuary, do it quietly.

3. Go back to the main assembly area without saying a word to anyone. Wait for the other students to assemble. When it is your turn, stand in the shape of a cross and all sing the first verse of "The Old Rugged Cross" to the rest of the group.

4. Have a spokesperson tell about the scripture passage and Jesus' obedience, even to death on the cross.

Obey C3
Obedience Team Ideas

- -

Moses and the Burning Bush

Read Exodus 3: 1 - 6. <u>Carefully follow these instructions:</u>
1. Answer among yourselves the following questions:
   How did Moses react when he saw the burning bush?
   What did God tell him? Why do you think God wanted him to take off his shoes?

Read Exodus 7:6.
   What does this verse say Moses and his brother, Aaron did?
   Would Moses have ever led the people out of slavery in Egypt if he hadn't obeyed God?

Read Exodus 20:1 - 17.
2. Have each of your team members take one or more of the "Ten Commandments" and memorize it. (memorize them in "one line" form - like "You shall not covet" and "You shall not make idols")

3. Go quietly back to the main assembly area. Wait for the other students to assemble. When it is your turn, stand in front of the group, take off your shoes, and, each taking a turn, quote the "Ten Commandments" in order.

4. Have a spokesperson tell about the scripture passages you studied and how important it was that Moses was obedient to God - and how important it is that we obey the "Ten Commandments".

Obey C4
Obedience Team Ideas

Noah and the Ark

Read Genesis 6: 9 - 22. <u>Carefully follow these instructions:</u>
1. Answer among yourselves the following questions:
   Why did God say he was going to flood the earth? Why did God choose Noah to build the ark? What was Noah's response, according to verse 22? What would have happened to Noah if he hadn't obeyed God and built the boat? What do you think Noah's neighbors thought of him building a boat in the desert?

2. Choose one of the following ways to demonstrate the ark:
   A. Make a scale drawing based on the dimensions given in the passage. Use a poster board and show the dimensions.

   B. Make a boat, using the poster board and tape.

3. Go quietly back to the assembly area. Wait for the other students to assemble. When it is your turn, make the outline of a boat on the floor in front of the group with your bodies.
Have a spokesperson tell the story of Noah and the importance of his obedience.

Obey C5
Obedience Team Ideas

Joshua Takes Jericho

Read Joshua 6:1 - 20. <u>Carefully follow these instructions:</u>

1. Answer among yourselves the following questions:
   How did God tell Joshua to attack the city?
   Why do you think God wanted Joshua to attack the city in such a strange way? What do you think Joshua thought of the strange plan?
   Would he have taken the city if he had not obeyed God?
   Do you think maybe God wanted to see if Joshua and the people would obey Him, no matter what? Do you think sometimes today God wants to see if we will obey Him, no matter what?

2. Go quietly back to the main assembly area. Wait for the other students to assemble. When it is your turn, stand and march around the rest of the group, blowing paper "trumpets" seven times. On the seventh time, shout "The Lord reigns" then run to your seats. Remain quietly in your seats.

3. Have a spokesperson tell the story found in these verses in his/her own words and talk about how we must obey God, no matter what, if we are going to win any victories in our lives.

Obey C6
Obedience Team Ideas

The Armor of God

Read Ephesians 6:10 - 18. <u>Carefully follow these instructions:</u>

1. Answer among yourselves the following questions:
Who is it that wars against us? How do we defend ourselves from them? What is the only <u>offensive</u> weapon named? What does Paul, the writer, mean by, "so that when the day of evil comes, you may be able to stand your ground, and after you have done everything, to stand" (verse 13)? Why does he tell us to *stand*?

2. Draw and cut each piece of the "armor of God" out of poster boards. Assign a student to hold and explain each one to the rest of the group when you get back together. (There are 6 pieces: a belt, breastplate, shoes, shield, helmet and sword.)

3. Go quietly back to the main assembly area. Wait for the other students to assemble. When it is your turn, stand and have the assigned students hold up and explain the pieces of armor to the group. After they have all done so, have every member of the team stand without a word for 2 full minutes. Try not to smile or move.

4. Have a spokesperson explain that you are "standing against the spiritual forces of this dark world".

Obey D

Cut along the dotted line. Make enough copies of this sheet to give to each student. Hand the sheets to the students at the end of the session.

- -

Obedience Rules!

There is a guy in the Bible who is never named - he is just "The man of God from Judah". He went up to Israel from Judah because God told him to. He stood before King Jeroboam and told him to straighten-up his act! King Jeroboam was evil in God's sight because he made two golden calves and had the people worship them instead of God.

Well, this un-named prophet stood up to him and told him he would lose his kingdom to one of David's descendants. The king yelled, "Seize him!", but his hand turned into a skeleton's hand when he pointed at the prophet. The prophet asked God to heal the hand, and so God did.

An old prophet, living in the area heard about this. He invited the guy to his home for dinner. But the prophet from Judah said, "No, the Lord told me not to eat or drink until I get back home to Judah." But the old prophet lied to him, "I am a prophet too, and God told me it would be okay for you to eat here tonight." (Yes, even men of God will let you down). The man from Judah thought, "okay". He rested there that night and ate and drank.

As he was going home the next day, a lion met him on the road and killed him. King Jeroboam never did repent and everything the prophet said about him came true. (See 1 Kings 13 and following.)

Even though the prophet was doing a good thing, and saying true words, he wasn't *completely* obedient to God and it cost him his life. God demands complete obedience from us - no matter whether or not it makes sense to us. We must remind ourselves that God is much smarter than we are and He *always* has in mind what is best for us. Do you have trouble obeying people who are in authority over you? If so, you probably have trouble obeying God, too. Pray that God will help you with this.

Obey E

Copy this sheet on colorful paper, then cut along the dotted lines to make door signs for the **obedience teams**.

TEAM #1

TEAM #2

TEAM #3

10

Session Ten: Witnessing Practice

A Peek at the Practice:
By the end of this session, you will have taught your students the importance of sharing their faith and will have led them to actually practice witnessing to one another.

The Primary Objective Points:

Students Will:

- Learn the importance of witnessing.
- Learn how to witness to others.
- Actually practice witnessing, using "role-play".

Plan Ahead:

Read through the lesson plan. Personalize it to fit your group's personality. Make any adjustments you deem necessary to fit the size and makeup of your group.

Make copies of the **prompt** question sheets (Witnessing B), then cut them into strips along the dotted lines. Make enough strips for each student. Have pens or pencils ready for each student's use.

Make enough copies of **Wrinkle-Free Witnessing** (Witnessing C) for each student.

Make enough copies of **Role Play Witnessing** (Witnessing D) for each student.

Pray for your students and for this session. Think about who won *you* to Christ. Think about some experiences you have had witnessing to others and about how it felt.

Set a chair by the doorway so students will pass by it as they enter. Place the **prompt** question strips on it. Tape the sign, "Please take a sheet and answer the question" (Witnessing A) on the back of the chair.

Practice Pointer:
The first nine sessions of this course will have prepared your students for this session. There are several memory verses here - but you should have already memorized most of them in session four. Also, your students have now practiced giving their testimonies and praying in front of others.

Prompt Your Young People:

As students enter the room, they will take a **prompt** question strip and answer the question. Take up the strips or have a volunteer do so.

Begin your session as you are most comfortable: Make needed announcements, sing songs, etc.

Next, take prayer requests. Pray, or call on someone to pray.

Sort through the **prompt** question strips and read some of the answers. Comment and allow the students to discuss their answers.

Point out that no one is saved unless someone tells him about the gospel. Tell the students about how you were saved and who told you the good news about Christ. (Of course, it could have been the work of several people - "I planted the seed, Apollos watered it, but God made it grow." **(1 Corinthians 3:6)**.

Preface the Practice:

Ask: "So, would *anyone* ever become a Christian if someone didn't tell him or her about Jesus and how to be saved?"

Explain that no one would ever be saved if another person didn't tell him about Christ. People have heard the good news in lots of different ways - but ultimately, it boils down to someone telling them.

> Paul said in **Romans 10:14**, "How can they call on the one they have not believed in? And how can they believe in one of whom they have not heard? And how can they hear without someone preaching to them?"

Ask: "The last thing Jesus told his disciples before he returned to heaven was to 'therefore go and make disciples of all nations'. Why did Jesus think it was so important that we tell others about Him?"

Explain that we are now "Jesus in the skin" - we are the only Jesus people will see. We have to take the good news to all people. Jesus left us with this great task - and this great honor.

> **Practice Pointer:**
> At this time, we will depart from the usual format. Hand out **Witnessing C, Wrinkle-Free Witnessing,** to each student, then continue by going over the next 3 pages.

So how do we witness to someone? Here are some basics of witnessing to keep in mind:

1) You have to walk the talk - you cannot witness to someone if you don't live any better than he does.

2) Nervousness is normal. Keep in mind that it's okay to be nervous - just don't let that stop you.

3) Be yourself - don't try to be someone you are not or talk in a way that's just not you.

4) Don't get bogged down in "unwinnable" debates. Just present the gospel clearly and as you understand it. Rely on the scripture and emphasize what is happening in your own life.

5) You must be their friend first. Take care of their physical and emotional needs (within reason). You cannot witness to a starving person and expect much response until you have helped him.

6) Let God do his job. The Holy Spirit makes a person realize he needs to be saved, and God actually saves him - it's just your job to tell him the truth of the good news.

All Christians should memorize the Gospel plan. It is a basic formula by which anyone can be saved:

1) You must **Realize** you are a sinner who needs to be saved - and that you cannot save yourself.

2) You must **Repent** of that sin and turn to Christ for forgiveness.

3) You must **Receive** Christ as your one and only savior.

This is such a simple, wonderful plan, but it cost Jesus his life. It's free but it's not cheap. It's free to us for the taking, but it cost God dearly. Let's look at it a little more closely and add some scripture.

First, you must come to the place where you realize that you have sinned and that sin separates you from God and will send you to hell when you die. **Romans 3:23** says, "for all have sinned and fall short of the glory of God." **Romans 6:23a** says, "for the wages of sin is death..." This means that the cost or payment for sin is death (and death here is separation from God - which is what Hell is.)

Second, you must turn from that sin. This means you feel sorry for it. You then ask Jesus to forgive you and "cleanse" you from sin. **1 John 1:9** says, "if we confess our sins, he is faithful and just and will forgive us our sins and purify us from all unrighteousness."

Third, you must admit that Jesus is the only way to heaven and He can and will save you. You must believe that He is God's son. You then simply ask him to save you (and mean it!) **Romans 10:13** says, "Everyone who calls on the name of the Lord will be saved."

You need to have a few scriptures memorized and marked in your Bible. Many call these the **Roman Road** because they are from the book of Romans:

> **Romans 3:23.** It tells us that we are *all* sinners.
> **Romans 6:23a.** It tells us what the penalty for that sin is.
> **Romans 6:23b.** It gives us hope, knowing that we can be saved from that penalty.
> **Romans 5:8**. It tells us that Christ died for us while we were still sinners.
> **Romans 10:9**. It says we must confess Jesus to others.
> **Romans 10:13**. It assures that whoever asks Jesus to save him will be saved.

Other important salvation verses are: **John 3:16.** Most people already know this verse. It's a great place to start. **John 14:6**, which says Jesus is the only way to be saved; **1 John 1:9**, which says God will forgive us if we ask him to; **Ephesians 2:8,9,** which says that we cannot save ourselves - we cannot *earn* our salvation - but that it is a free gift from God because he loves us and must simply have faith in Him.

You will witness to **four** basic types of people:
1) **The Spiritually Apathetic.**
   This person just doesn't believe the Bible is true or that Jesus is who he said he is. Much prayer and patience is needed here.
2) **The Spiritually Ignorant.**
   This person has been taught - but wrongly. He may be a member of a cult or false religion. You will need to know the truth well to win him. This takes a lot of prayer and a non-combative attitude.
3) **The Spiritually Innocent.**
   This person just doesn't know the good news that Jesus died for him.

4) The Spiritually Ripe.
This person has heard or wants to hear. He is ready to be saved.

In dealing with all of these types of people, it is important to remember that:
1) God's word has power - let it do the work.
2) Don't be argumentative. Show kindness, love and understanding.
3) Emphasize your own testimony. What has God done for you?
4) The Holy Spirit is the one who saves, not you. Let Him guide you.
   (In other words, be in an attitude of prayer as you witness.)

A Promise to Ponder:
" ...So is my word that goes out from my mouth: It will not return to me empty, but will accomplish what I desire and achieve the purpose for which I sent it." **Isaiah 55:11**

Practice Makes Perfect:

Explain to the students that at this time you are going to practice witnessing to each other. For the purposes of this exercise, you will "role play" witnessing. The person being witnessed to will be **spiritually innocent** and **spiritually ripe** - in other words, this will not be a time for arguing, debating, or asking difficult questions, but will be an exercise in winning a person to Christ who is ready to be saved.

Explain to the students that after the first student has practiced witnessing to his partner, the students can **switch places** and the other student will practice witnessing. Encourage the students to try it *without* using the **Role Play Witnessing** sheets after they have gone through it with it.

It may be helpful for you to select a volunteer and personally demonstrate how this will work. Get the volunteer to sit or stand with you and you "win" him or her to the Lord.

Tell the students to select partners. They will pull their chairs together, facing each other, then decide which one will witness and which one will be "saved". *Person One will need to have a Bible.* Instruct the students to carry the "role play" all the way through so that the "lost" person asks Jesus into his heart and becomes a Christian.

Practice Pointer:
You may want to make sure two "lost" students don't pair up. This may not be avoidable, and that is okay, but ideally you want at least one Christian student in each pair. Also, allow three or more to stay together for this practice at your discretion, but again, two is more ideal.

Practice Pointer:
You may feel a little uncomfortable with the thought of role-playing such a serious issue as salvation, but it is important for your students to get a chance to practice witnessing to each other. This shouldn't, however, be handled in a frivolous or disrespectful way.

If you have time, get the students to find another partner and practice again.

A Post-Practice Postlude:

Get the students to turn their chairs back toward the front. Ask how it went. See if there are any questions, comments or problems you need to address. Ask if anyone *actually* just asked Jesus into his heart and became a Christian. If so, congratulate and encourage him and follow-up on his decision.

If you have time, you may ask one or more of the pairs to go through the role-play in front of the rest of the students.

Remember to always encourage your students and be careful not to criticize them.

Pray or call on someone to pray. Dismiss.

Witnessing A

Cut along the dotted line to make a "prompt instruction" sign: place this sign on the back of a chair near the doorway, with slips of paper with the **prompt** question on them. Make sure pens or pencils are available.

Please Take A Slip of Paper and Answer the Question!

Witnessing B

Make enough copies of this page so each student can get a slip of paper with the **prompt** question on it as they enter the room. Then cut along the dotted lines to make the slips.

Please name the person who was preaching or speaking when you became a Christian. Where were you?

Please name the person who was preaching or speaking when you became a Christian. Where were you?

Please name the person who was preaching or speaking when you became a Christian. Where were you?

Witnessing C

Make enough copies for each student then hand them out during the **Preface the Practice** part of the session.

Wrinkle-Free Witnessing

The Basics of Witnessing

1. Walk the Talk.
2. Nervousness is Natural.
3. Be yourself.
4. Don't get "bogged down".
5. Be their friend first.
6. Let God do his Job.

The Plan of Salvation

1. You must **Realize** that you are a sinner who needs to be saved.
   Romans 3:23, Romans 6:23a

2. You must **Repent** of that sin and turn to Christ for forgiveness.
   Romans 6:23b, 1 John 1:9

3. You must **Receive** Christ as your one and only savior.
   John 14:6, John 3:16, Romans 10:9,10,13

You must acknowledge that Jesus is God, that He rose from the dead and that He and only He can save you. You cannot save yourself by doing good or going to church.
(Ephesians 2:8,9)

After you are saved, you need to confess Jesus to others and be Baptized. Then you need to walk with God everyday - that is what He created you for! You do this by reading your Bible, Praying and hanging out with other Christians - like at Church.

Witnessing D

Make enough copies of this sheet for each student.
Hand this out for **Practice Makes Perfect** and have
the students use it to practice witnessing to one another.

Role Play Witnessing

Person One: Is saved and will help person two become a Christian.
Person Two: Is lost but wants to become a Christian - just needs to know how.

Person One:
   Ask the following questions:

   If you died today, do you think you would go to Heaven or Hell?
   (Let Person Two answer.)
   Why do you believe this?
   (Let Person Two answer.)

Person One:
   Say: "This is what the Bible says."
   (Elaborate as much as you want, but read the scriptures.)
   1. You are a sinner. (Romans 3:23)
   2. Being a sinner will send you to Hell. (Romans 6:23a)
   3. You cannot save yourself. (Ephesians 2:8,9)
   4. Jesus can and will save you if you let Him.
                                        (Romans 10:13)
   Ask: "Do you have any questions?" **(Let him or her answer.)**
   Ask: "Would you like to become a Christian?"

Person Two: Say: "Yes, I would!"

Person One: Say: "Repeat after me as I lead in prayer - and remember, you have to really mean it!" **(Person Two will repeat each phrase)**
   Lord Jesus, **(repeat)** I know I am a sinner, **(repeat)** and I cannot save my self by being good. **(repeat)** I believe Jesus died on the cross for my sins, **(repeat)** and rose from the dead. **(repeat)** I ask you now to forgive me of my sins. **(repeat)** I ask you to come into my heart, **(repeat)** and to save me. **(repeat)**. And from this day forward **(repeat)** I will live for you. **(repeat)**   In Jesus' name I pray, Amen. **(repeat)**.

A note from the author:

So now what? You have taken your students through this course with the thought, "practice makes perfect", in mind.

Now, think of another phrase, "use it or lose it".

Think of ways to encourage and enable your students to *use* what they have learned. They need to continue to practice witnessing, giving their testimonies, praying aloud and participating in the other tenets of the faith. Let your students give their testimonies on a regular basis; take them witnessing - like on mission trips or to the mall; let them teach; call on them to quote scriptures they have learned; let them sing in front of the group and the church.

Then, after about a year has passed, take them through this course again.

God bless you and your ministry.